Childcraft

The How and Why Library

Volume 7

How Things Work

World Book, Inc.

a Scott Fetzer company

Chicago London Sydney Toronto

1988 Edition
Childcraft—The How and Why Library
(Reg. U.S. Pat. Off.)
Copyright © 1987, U.S.A. by World Book, Inc.
Merchandise Mart Plaza, Chicago, Illinois 60654
All rights reserved.
This volume may not be reproduced in whole or in part in
any form without written permission from the publishers.
Copyright © 1986, 1985 by World Book, Inc.
Copyright © 1982, 1981, 1980, 1979, U.S.A. by World
Book-Childcraft International, Inc. Copyright © 1976, 1974,
1973, 1971, 1970, 1969, 1968, 1965, 1964, U.S.A. by Field
Enterprises Educational Corporation.
International Copyright © 1987, 1986, 1985 by World Book,
Inc. International Copyright © 1982, 1981, 1980, 1979, by
World Book-Childcraft International, Inc.; International Copy-
right © 1976, 1974, 1973, 1971, 1970, 1969, 1968, 1965,
1964, by Field Enterprises Educational Corporation.
Printed in the United States of America
ISBN 0-7166-0188-5
Library of Congress Catalog Card No. 87-50086

Acknowledgments

The publishers of *Childcraft—The How and Why Library*
gratefully acknowledge the courtesy of the following
publishers, agencies, and corporations for permission to
use copyrighted stories, poems, and other material in this volume.
Full illustration acknowledgments appear on pages 329–330.

Cricket Magazine: The wind skipper toy adapted from *Cricket
Magazine*

Houghton Mifflin Company: ''I Met a Man I Could Not See,'' from *I
Met a Man* by John Ciardi, published by Houghton Mifflin Company.
Copyright © 1961 by John Ciardi. Reprinted by permission.

Little, Brown and Company: ''The Lightning Rods,'' from *Ben and
Me* by Robert Lawson. Copyright © 1939 by Robert Lawson.
Copyright renewed © 1966 by John W. Boyd. Reprinted by
permission of Little, Brown and Company.

Western Publishing Company, Inc.: ''Hump, the Escalator'' by
Dorothy Faubion. Copyright 1942 by Story Parade, Inc. Reprinted by
permission of Western Publishing Company, Inc.

Volume 7

How Things Work

Contents

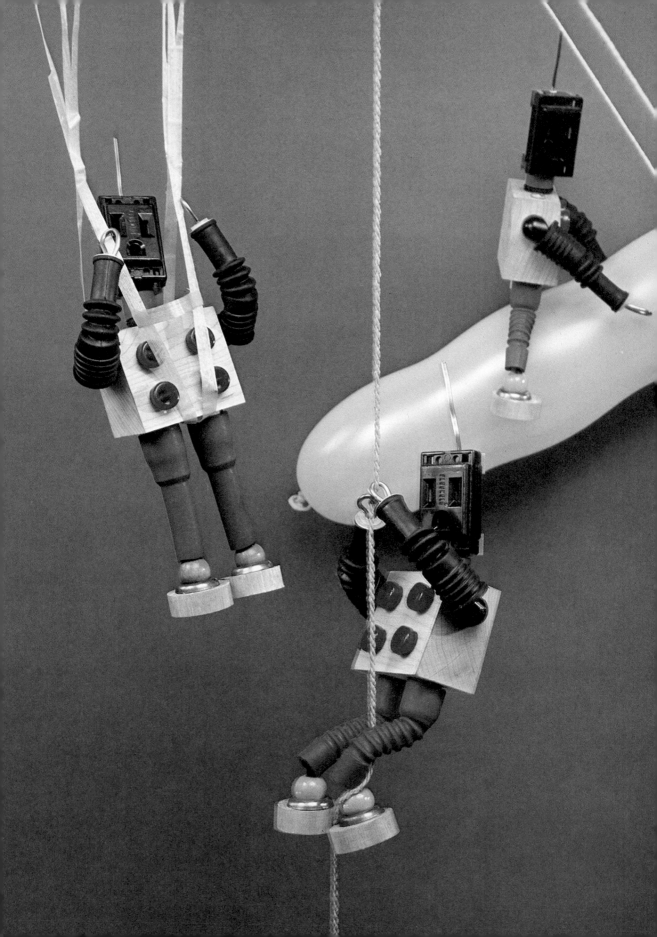

Let's Get Moving

Pushes and pulls

Back and forth, up and down. Swinging in a swing is almost like flying. What makes the swing go up in the air?

Most of the time you do. You "pump" with your legs and body. Sometimes you can get a friend to push you. And sometimes you see the empty swing moving when the wind pushes it. But something—you, your friend, or the wind—has to give it a push. The swing can't move by itself.

Anytime a thing moves, something *makes* it move. Something pushes it, the way you, your friend, or the wind pushes the swing. Or something pulls it, the way you pull a wagon or a sled. The push or the pull that makes a thing move is called a *force*.

Seesaws and swings, roller skates and bicycles all get their force from you. Pushes from your hands and feet make them move, carrying you up and down through the air or whizzing you along on the ground.

The invisible push

The light turns green and the car starts to move quickly. It feels as if a big, invisible hand pushes you back in the car seat and makes you stay there. But it feels different when the car stops quickly. The same "hand" seems to give you an invisible push forward. It feels as if the "hand" wants you to keep going. If you didn't have a seat belt on, you might hit the front window.

What is this invisible "something" that pushes you when a car starts and stops? It's called *inertia* (ihn UR shuh).

Inertia is a name for the way things behave when they are stopped and when they are moving. When anything is stopped, it *stays* stopped—it can't start moving by itself. It

only starts to move when a force—a push or a pull—makes it move. And when anything is moving, it tries to *keep* moving. It won't stop until a force stops it.

When a car starts to move, your body tries to stay stopped. So you feel yourself pressing back as the car seat moves forward. And when the car stops, your body tries to keep moving. Inertia "pushes" you forward. Your seat belt is there to hold you back.

Here's a little trick you can do with inertia. Lay a playing card over a drinking glass. Put a penny on the card. Very quickly, pull the card off the glass, straight toward you.

You might think the penny would "ride" along on the card. But it won't. Inertia keeps it from moving. It will stay where it is—and drop into the glass with a clink.

How do brakes work?

Slow down! There's a busy street ahead. Stop your bike and wait for the traffic light to change. Then you can cross safely.

Your bike's brakes are there to help you stop. When you squeeze the levers on the handlebars, the brakes rub against the wheels and slow the bike down.

The rubbing that you use to stop is called *friction* (FRIHK shuhn). Friction is what makes moving things slow down.

If the brakes and wheels were perfectly smooth, they would slide over each other easily, without rubbing. Your bike would keep moving.

But nothing is *perfectly* smooth. Even shiny, polished things are covered with tiny rough spots. When one object slides across another, the rough spots rub against each other. Friction—the rubbing of the rough spots—makes things move more and more slowly, until finally they stop. And that's how brakes work.

This bicycle has hand brakes—one for the front wheel and one for the rear wheel. To stop, the rider squeezes the levers on the handle bars.

When the bicycle is moving, the brake pads don't touch the wheel (left). But when the rider squeezes the brake handle, the pads rub against the rim of the wheel (right). This makes the wheel stop turning.

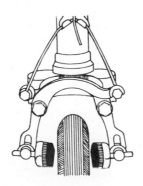
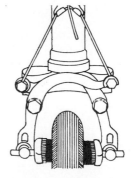

Friction from air

Even air creates friction—it rubs against moving things and slows them down. You can make a "helicopter" that uses the friction of air to slow its fall—and to spin, too.

Place the paper with the short edge toward you. Fold the paper in half the long way. Open the paper. Fold the bottom corners in until they meet at the center crease. You will have two folded triangles at the bottom of the paper. Next, fold the outer edge of each triangle in as far as the center crease.

Hold the folded paper straight up and down. Let it drop. Does it fall fast or slowly? Here is something you can do to slow it down.

Measure one inch (2.5 centimeters) up the center crease from where the folded edges meet and make a mark. Cut along the crease from the top down to the mark. Fold the paper on one side of the cut forward. Fold the other side back. Now your "helicopter" has flaps.

Drop your "helicopter" again. This time it falls gently, spinning as it goes. The air rubbing and pushing on the two flaps makes all the difference.

Materials

- paper (8½ x 11 inches; 21.5 x 27.5 centimeters)
- ruler
- scissors

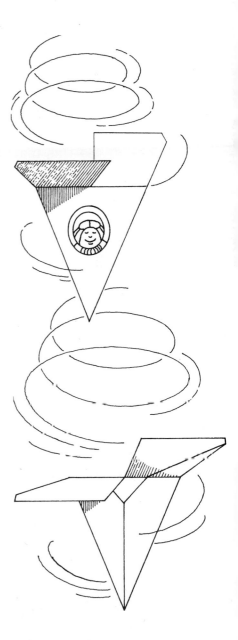

A machine that never stops?

For twenty-seven years Dr. Coatsworthy Mothbold has been building an automatic polka-dotting machine. It can paint polka dots on anything—walls and windows, shirts and socks, even pretzels and pancakes!

Best of all, the polka-dotter is a perpetual-motion machine! Perpetual motion (puhr PEHCH u uhl MOH shuhn) is motion that goes on forever. So this machine, says Dr. Mothbold proudly, will never stop!

All the parts of the polka-dotter create forces—pushes and pulls—that make the other parts work. And as each part gets a push or pull, it gives a push or pull to another part. So Dr. Mothbold is sure the machine will keep running itself. Is Dr. Mothbold right?

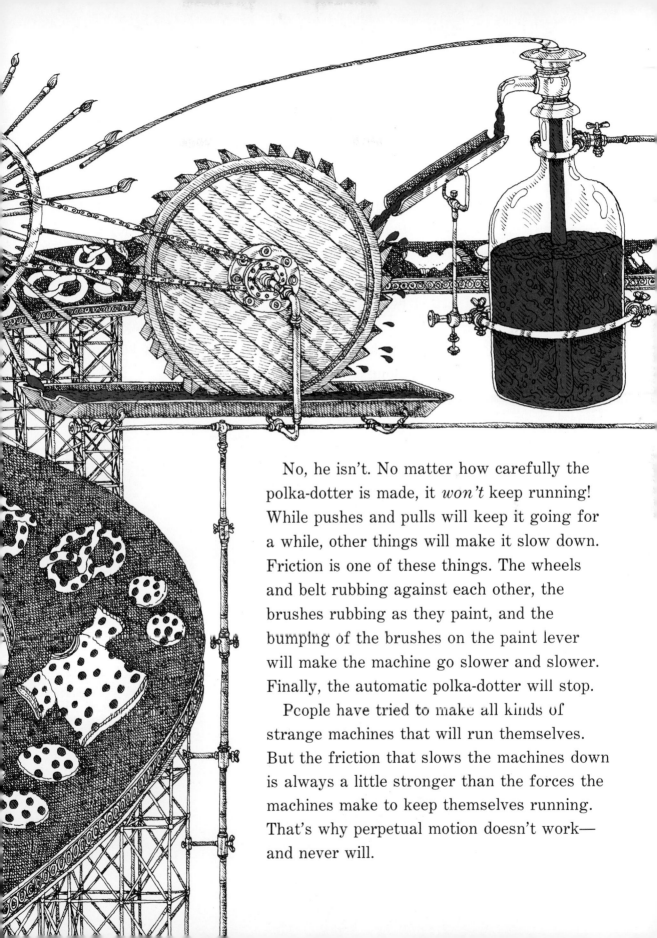

No, he isn't. No matter how carefully the polka-dotter is made, it *won't* keep running! While pushes and pulls will keep it going for a while, other things will make it slow down. Friction is one of these things. The wheels and belt rubbing against each other, the brushes rubbing as they paint, and the bumping of the brushes on the paint lever will make the machine go slower and slower. Finally, the automatic polka-dotter will stop.

People have tried to make all kinds of strange machines that will run themselves. But the friction that slows the machines down is always a little stronger than the forces the machines make to keep themselves running. That's why perpetual motion doesn't work— and never will.

A force that pushes and pulls

Magnets can do strange things—that's what makes them such fun to play with. They can stick to each other. They can make nails or pins hang on to each other, like people holding hands. They can even "lead" each other across a piece of glass. The magnet on top of the glass follows the magnet you pull along under the glass.

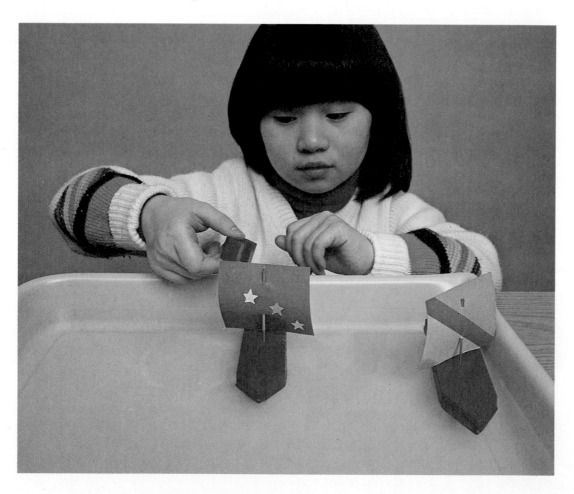

A special force, or pull, makes a magnet work. The pull is strongest in two places called *poles*—a north pole and a south pole.

Either pole of a magnet will hang on to iron and steel things, like pans and pins. And either pole will hang on to *one* pole of another magnet. The north pole of one magnet and the south pole of the other will pull on each other and make the magnets stick together like best friends.

But magnets stick together only if the poles don't match. If you put two north poles or two south poles together, the magnets try to push each other away!

Magnet power

You can use a magnet to make another magnet. First pick the pole that you will use. Make sure you use only one pole.

Hold the needle in one hand. Rub the end of the magnet from the needle's eye to the tip. Always rub in only *one* direction.

After fifty rubs, test the needle to see if it has a pull. Will it pick up a pin? How many pins will it hold? What will it stick to?

Rub the needle fifty more times to make the pull stronger. Then stick the needle in a small piece of wood to make a boat.

Put your boat in a pan of water. Then use the poles of the big magnet to push and pull the boat, so that it "sails" across the pan.

Materials
- magnet
- needle (large)
- pins
- wood (small piece)

A tug from the earth

Imagine floating through the air, standing on the ceiling, or leaping upstairs in one big bound! An astronaut traveling through space can do all of these things. But on the earth, you can't.

You can't do these things on earth because a special kind of force tugs on you and keeps your feet on the floor. This force is called *gravity* (GRAV uh tee). Gravity is the pull that makes things slide or fall or roll downward.

As long as you are on the earth, the tug of the earth's gravity pulls on you and everything else. When you let go of a ball, it falls to the ground. When you jump, you come back down to the earth instead of flying into the air.

A spaceship can travel beyond the reach of the earth's gravity. So on a space flight away from the earth, you'll reach a place where there is no gravity—the earth isn't tugging on you at all.

What will happen then? You'll float, unless you hang on! Anything you "drop" will float in the air when you let go of it. And if you jump, you won't come down—you'll hit your head on the ceiling, instead.

This astronaut is too far from earth to feel the pull of gravity. So, on a "walk" outside the spaceship, he floats instead of falling. The tube is attached to the ship to keep him from floating away.

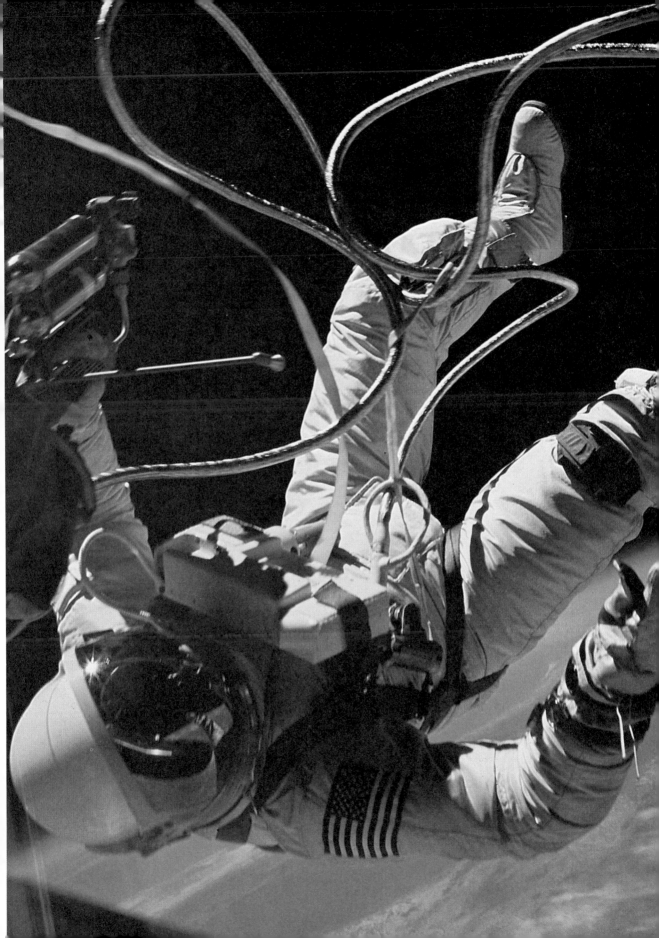

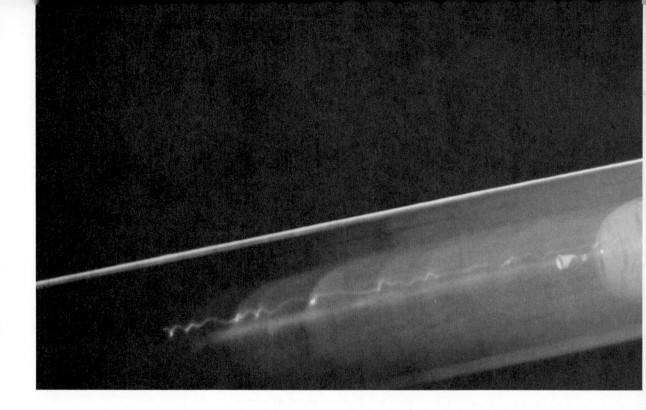

A push in two directions

Blowing up a balloon takes a lot of huffing and puffing. But if you let the balloon go, the air rushes out—and the balloon takes off like a rocket! What makes it fly?

When you blow up a balloon, you push air into it. The force, or push, of the air inside the balloon makes the balloon bigger.

But anytime something makes a push, the thing it pushes against pushes back. The two pushes are exactly the same size, but they go in opposite directions.

The air inside is pushing on the balloon, but the balloon is pushing on the air, too. When you let go, the balloon pushes the air out of the opening. But the air pushes back at the balloon—and the push makes the balloon fly.

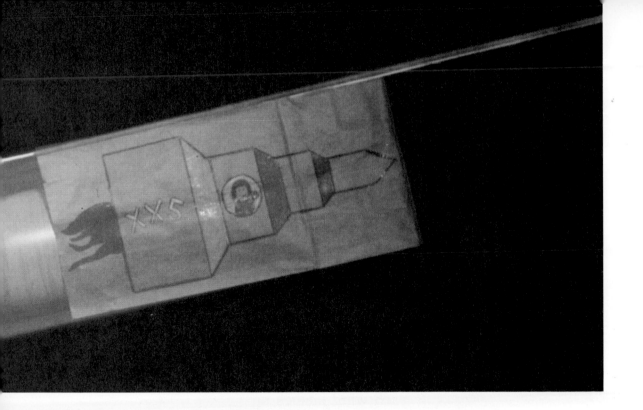

A rocket balloon

This project proves that when there is a push in one direction, there is always an equal push in the opposite direction.

Flatten the bag. Place the straw on the middle of one side, along the length of the bag. Tape the straw to the bag. Decorate the bag to look like a rocket, using the side with the straw as the top.

Thread the string through the straw. Then stretch the string between two chairs. Tie the ends so that the string is tight. Slide the straw to one end of the string.

Slip the balloon into the bag. Then blow up the balloon. Now your rocket is ready to fly.

Let go of the balloon. Your rocket will take off and zip forward along the string, pushed by the air rushing out of the balloon.

Materials

- balloon (long)
- crayons
- drinking straw (long)
- paper bag (small)
- string (long)
- tape

What keeps them up?

How do an airplane's wings help it stay in the air? What keeps a satellite up?

Airplane wings have a special shape. They are curved on top and straight on the bottom. This shape is what helps lift the plane up.

When the plane starts to move, the wings cut through the air. The air moves over the curved top of the wing and under the straight bottom. The air moving over each wing pushes down on it. And the air moving under each wing pushes up.

The curved top of the wing is longer than the straight bottom. The air moving over the wing has to travel farther than air moving under it. So the air going over the wing moves faster. And the faster it moves, the less it pushes. As the push *over* the wing gets weaker, the push *under* the wing begins to lift the plane. So the plane leaves the ground. As long as the plane keeps moving, the wings lift it and help it to fly.

Far out in space, a satellite circles the earth. What keeps it from falling? And what keeps it from sailing away?

Two kinds of forces work to make the satellite circle around the earth. One is the tremendous push of the satellite's speed—thousands of miles (kilometers) per hour. Without this push, gravity would pull the satellite back to earth.

The shape of the wings
helps an airplane to fly.

The other force is the pull of the earth's
gravity, which reaches far out into space.
Without this pull, a satellite would travel in a
straight line, away from the earth.

Gravity pulls the satellite toward the earth.
But the speed of the satellite pushes it
outward. When the push and the pull are
even, the satellite can't sail away from the
earth—or fall back to the earth, either.
Instead, it speeds *around* the earth, making
a circle in space.

Full of Energy

How do you make a push?

Opening doors, playing baseball, running a race, practicing for a school play—you really keep moving. How does your body keep going? What makes you move?

You keep moving in almost the same way a car keeps running. Both you and the car use forces—pushes and pulls—to move. And those forces have to come from something. What you and the car need is energy! Energy is what gives things the power that makes them work. It makes the pushes and pulls happen.

Your body gets its energy from food. It takes a scrambled egg or a plate of spaghetti and breaks it down, or digests it. The energy you get from digested food makes the pushes and pulls that keep you moving.

A car engine burns gasoline to keep running. As the gasoline burns, it gives off energy. That energy makes the pushes and pulls that turn the wheels.

You can't run on gasoline, and the car can't run on scrambled eggs. But you and the car really are using energy in much the same way. What's more, the energy you and the car use comes from the same place. It comes from the sun!

Food is made from plants and animals. All

plants and animals store up energy from the sun as they live and grow, and you get that energy when you eat.

Gasoline is made from oil. And oil comes from plants and animals, too. Those plants and animals lived millions of years ago, storing up energy from the sun just as living things do today. So when a car burns gasoline, it's using energy from the sun— energy that has been stored inside the earth for millions of years.

Energy from movement

Poor old Bristlebones! His pirate ship has sailed away and he's stranded on a tiny island. He can think of only three ways to get help. He can fly a kite and hope somebody on another ship sees it. He can put a message in a bottle and let it float away in the ocean for someone to find. Or he can build a raft with a sail and try to get away.

Each of Bristlebones' ideas depends on a kind of energy to work—the movement of wind to lift a kite or push a sail, or the movement of water to carry a bottle. Moving things like wind and water have energy that can be used to give something else a push or a pull. This kind of energy is called kinetic (kih NEHT ihk) energy. *Kinetic* comes from a Greek word for "move." Kinetic energy is the energy of moving things.

Anything that is moving has kinetic energy—even the coconuts that fall from the trees on Bristlebones' island. While the coconuts are falling, they have kinetic energy. They can give quite a push to anything they hit, including Bristlebones' head!

But even before the coconuts fall, they have another kind of energy. They aren't moving, so it isn't kinetic energy. But they *could* move—they could fall. The coconuts in the tree have what is called potential energy. *Potential* means "possible." Potential energy

is often called "stored energy"—energy that *could* be used.

The coconuts on the tree have potential energy. On the ground, they have no energy at all—they aren't moving, and they can't move. But if Bristlebones picks one up, it has potential energy again—it could be made to move by dropping it, rolling it, or throwing it.

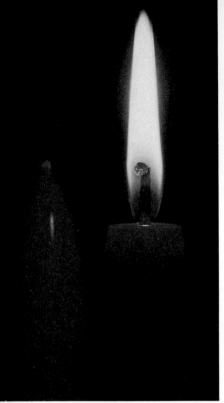

a wax candle

a coal fire

Energy from burning

Little Nancy Etticoat,
With a white petticoat,
And a red nose;
She has no feet or hands,
The longer she stands,
The shorter she grows.

Mother Goose

Who is Nancy Etticoat? You've seen her often, especially on birthdays. She's a candle! The "petticoat" is the melting wax, and the "red nose" is the flame. And a candle certainly gets shorter! The wax is used up as the candle burns.

The candle wax has a kind of stored-up energy. It's a fuel (FYOO uhl). A fuel is

an oil-burning lamp

a wood fire

something that is burned to make light, heat, or a push that makes things move. The coal, oil, and gas used to heat houses are all fuels. So is the gasoline in a car or the wood in a fireplace.

The same thing happens to every kind of fuel when it burns. When it starts burning, the heat makes it break down and change to other things, such as ashes. As the fuel breaks down, it gives off energy. Some of the energy is light, and some is heat.

When oil or gasoline is burned in a car engine, the heat energy makes the engine push—and the push from the engine makes the car run.

The energy stored in a fuel is called chemical (KEHM uh kuhl) energy.

Energy from electricity

Snorkel and Scorch are terribly sad. For two hundred years they worked as palace dragons. They carried wood for fires, huffed flames into fireplaces, and lighted candles in the palace halls. But now they are out of work.

It isn't their fault. Things at the palace have changed. Now the royal halls are lit with light bulbs, and the rooms are heated with a furnace. There is even a brand-new stove in the kitchen.

Electricity (ih lehk TRIHS uh tee) is doing the work that Snorkel and Scorch used to do.

Electricity is one kind of energy. It is a current that flows through a wire, much as water flows through a hose. An electric current can do the same kind of work a fuel can do. It can make light and heat. And it can make the push or pull that runs a machine.

So Snorkel and Scorch don't have to carry wood, light fires, or keep the candles burning any more. All they have to do is push the switches that turn the electric current on and off. Life will be much easier from now on—and Snorkel and Scorch will have enough free time to help out at palace picnics and barbecues.

Energy from the sun

Someday you may live in a house that keeps
itself warm with a tankful of "sunshine"—
even on cloudy days and chilly nights. Instead
of turning on a furnace, you'll use saved-up
heat from the sun.

The heat for such a house comes from solar
energy. *Sol* is the Latin word for "sun." So
solar (SOH luhr) energy is energy from the
sun. And a house that uses the sun's energy
is a solar house—a "sunshine house."

A solar house has special collectors to
capture the sun's heat. Usually the collectors
are built on the roof or on the sunniest side
of the house.

How is the sun's heat stored? In one kind
of solar house, water or another liquid is
pumped through the collectors on sunny days
to pick up heat. Next, the hot water is piped
to a huge tank of sand or gravel. Bit by bit,
it heats the whole tank. Sand or gravel can
hold heat longer than water does, so heat

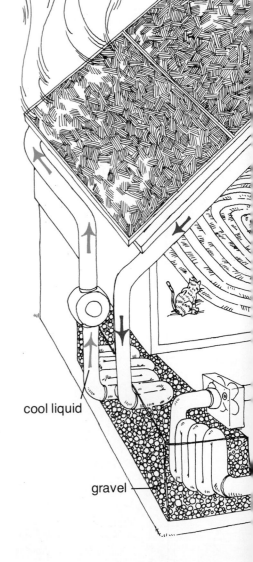

cool liquid

gravel

stays in the tank long after the sun goes down.

When the house is chilly, all you do is press a button that turns on a fan by the tank. The fan pulls the cool air into the hot tank. When the air gets warm, it is blown out of the tank and through the house. So the house gets warm, and you do, too—with a tankful of stored-up heat from the sun.

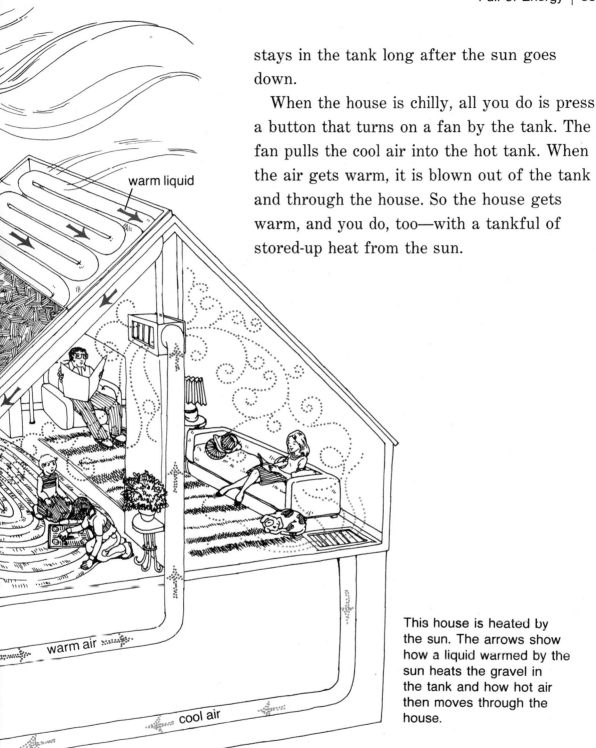

warm liquid

warm air

cool air

This house is heated by the sun. The arrows show how a liquid warmed by the sun heats the gravel in the tank and how hot air then moves through the house.

Energy from the wind

A push from the wind can make a kite fly and a sailboat glide across the water—and it can do other things, too. It can even light lamps and pump water!

If you live in a place where a strong, steady wind blows, you can use wind energy to pump water and make electricity for your home. A machine called a windmill uses the energy in the wind to do the work.

Windmills come in different shapes and sizes, but they are all alike in some ways. They have a wheel, which is the part that spins. And they are tall enough to catch the strong winds that blow high above the ground.

The wheel has paddles, sails, or blades for the wind to push against. When the wind blows, the wheel spins. This makes a push that runs a water pump or an electricity-making machine called a generator (JEHN uh ray tuhr).

Of course, the wind doesn't always blow, so sometimes the windmill doesn't run. But water pumped by the windmill can be stored in tanks. And electricity made when the windmill runs can be stored in batteries. Until the windmill goes back to work, you can use stored-up water and stored-up electricity in your home.

These scientists are testing a new kind of wind machine. The special curved shape makes the blades spin easily in the wind.

old windmills used to grind grain

a windmill used to pump water

a propeller-type windmill on the roof of a city building, used to make electricity

Energy from sound

Beneath the fishing boat there are thousands of fish waiting to be caught. The crew on the boat can't see the fish—but they know the fish are there. How can they tell?

There is a special kind of "whistle" that can help people find fish. It's ultrasound—sound that is higher than any sound your

ears can hear. Ultrasound can be used underwater to find things that people can't see.

All sounds—even the ones you can't hear—are actually bunches of tiny pushes and pulls. Those pushes and pulls make waves that can travel through things like water, air, and even the ground. The waves are a kind of energy—sound energy.

The "whistle" that finds fish is made by a special machine called a sonar (SOH nahr). The sonar sends ultrasound waves through the water in a narrow beam. It makes the beam sweep in a big circle around the boat.

Whenever the beam of ultrasound hits something, it bounces back to the sonar. Then the sonar signals that there is something in that spot. Usually the signal shows the bottom of the lake or river. But once in a while the beam hits something else.

The "something" in that spot could be rocks, a bed of seaweed, or fish. Rocks and seaweed stay in one place, so the signal from a rock pile or a seaweed bed always stays the same. But fish move—so a signal that keeps changing almost always means a school of swimming fish!

Of course, ultrasound won't make the fish bite on a hook or swim into the net of a big fishing boat. But it shows where the fish are—and it makes your chances for a fish dinner a lot better!

Energy from atoms

What's the smallest bit of something you can imagine? Is it a cookie crumb? Is it a pinpoint? Maybe it's the period at the end of this sentence.

Actually, all things—even you—are made up of billions and billions of "bits" even smaller than any of these things. These "bits" are atoms (AT uhmz). Atoms are so tiny that your eyes can't see them. They can only be seen with a special, tremendously powerful microscope.

Atoms are the tiniest pieces that things can be broken into and still stay the same. One atom of gold is the tiniest bit of gold possible—but it's still the same as all the gold in a ring or a royal crown. And one atom of oxygen is the tiniest bit of oxygen possible—but it's the same as all the oxygen in the air you breathe.

Atoms can be split into even smaller pieces. But if atoms split, they change into something else! When a very big atom, like a uranium (yu RAY nee uhm) atom, is split up, it isn't the same kind of atom any more. The biggest pieces of the atom turn into other smaller kinds of atoms. Some very tiny pieces of the uranium atom fly off into space. And something else is given off, too—energy!

The energy that comes from splitting atoms is usually called nuclear (NOO klee uhr)

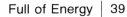

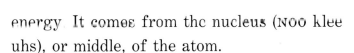

energy. It comes from the nucleus (NOO klee uhs), or middle, of the atom.

A special kind of machine can split atoms to make nuclear energy. The atoms don't burn when they are split. But they do give off a tremendous amount of heat. So a machine that splits atoms can be used the same way a fuel-burning engine is used. The machine makes heat. The heat makes a push—and the push makes other machines run.

Changing energy

Crack! It's a home run—and it was scored by a hamburger!

It's true that the hamburger didn't hit the ball. The batter did. But the batter ate the hamburger for lunch. The batter's body got energy from the hamburger. Some of this energy was used to swing the bat. And the energy in the swinging bat knocked the ball over the fence. So stand up and cheer for the hamburger—it scored the home run!

There are only a few kinds of energy. But each kind of energy can change into other kinds. Chemical energy in the food you eat can be changed into kinetic energy when you run or hit a ball. And other energy changes can be used to make other things work.

Here are two moving toys you can make that use energy in different ways. The first toy gets energy from something else that moves—the wind. But the second one works when heat energy changes into the energy of moving things.

Materials:
- cardboard (thin)
- paste
- pencil
- scissors
- tracing paper

A wind-skipper

This toy doesn't fly like a kite. But it will skip and spin down a sidewalk on a breezy day.

Fold the tracing paper in half. Place the folded edge along the dotted line and trace

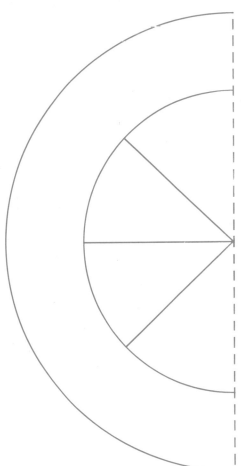

the half-pattern shown here. Turn the folded
paper over and trace the other half. Open the
paper and paste it on the cardboard. Then cut
out the pattern.

First, cut around the outside circle. Then
poke your scissors through the center. Cut
along each line just to the inner circle.

Next bend the points as shown here—one
up, one down, until you have gone all around
the circle.

Set your wind-skipper on the sidewalk. The
eight points will act like small sails. They will
catch a push from the wind, and the wind-
skipper will twirl along the ground.

A snake-dancer

Materials:

- construction paper
- needle
- pencil (unsharpened, with eraser)
- scissors
- spool
- thimble
- tracing paper

This snake is lazy when it's cold—but if you put it near something warm, it dances!

Trace the pattern shown here on the tracing paper. Paste the paper on the construction paper.

Cut around the outside of the shape. Then carefully poke your scissors through the center and cut out the circle. The hole should be big enough to fit over the thimble—if not, make it bigger. Then cut along the spiral line.

Push the thimble into the hole. Gently pull on the snake's head to make the spiral open up.

Stand the pencil in the spool, with the eraser up. If the pencil wobbles, stuff paper in the hole. Now poke the needle into the eraser. Hang the thimble over the needle, as shown here, to make the snake "stand."

Put your snake-dancer in a warm place—on a radiator, a fireplace mantel, or the top of a television set—or hold it over a burning light bulb. The heat makes the air move—and the moving air makes the snake-dancer spin around and around.

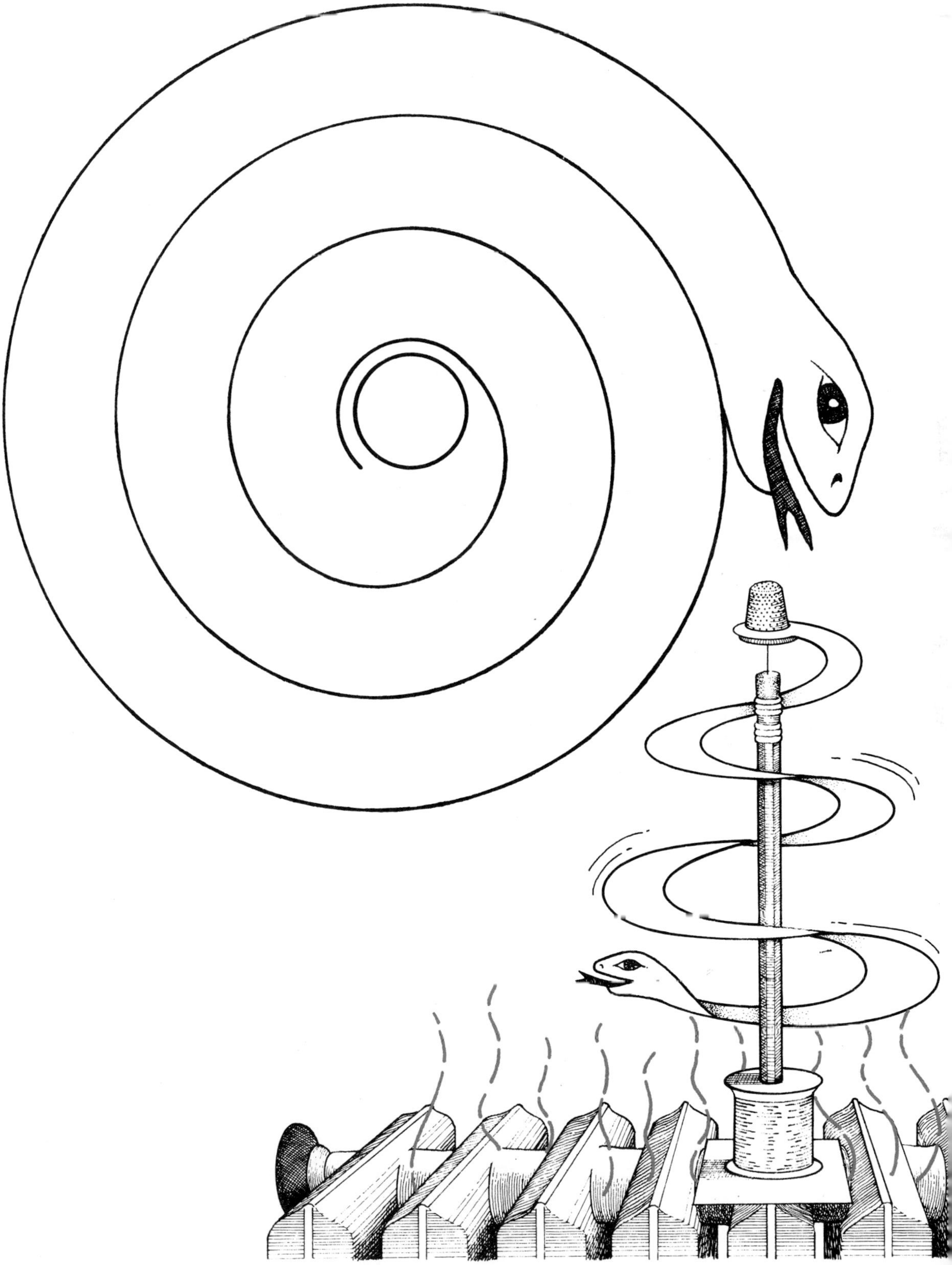

Where are the horses?

Imagine a team of horses—fifty or a hundred or even more—pulling your car down the highway! Actually, your car's engine has that much pulling power—the pulling power of a certain number of horses. And that's how its power is measured—in horsepower.

When engines were first used to run machines, people compared the power of an engine with the work a horse could do. An engine-maker would say that an engine could do the work of two horses, or pull as hard as a four-horse team.

But this was only a very rough measurement. Some horses pull harder than others. Until someone found a way to measure the power of an engine, no one could be sure that an engine was strong enough to do a job.

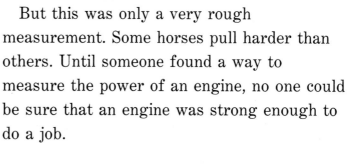

James Watt, an inventor, made some important improvements in engines. And he found a way to measure the real power of an engine.

First, Watt tested two strong workhorses to find out how much weight they could pull. He found that a good horse could pull 550 pounds (247.5 kilograms) one foot (30 centimeters) in one second. Next he measured the pull of engines. An engine that could do the same amount of work in one second as one horse could do was said to have one horsepower.

We still measure an engine's power this way. When we say that a car's engine has 150 horsepower, we mean that the engine can make a pull 150 times as strong as the one-horse pull James Watt measured. And the engine in a car takes up much less space than 150 horses!

Windwagon Smith

The story of Windwagon Smith is actually a "tall tale" that was made up by American frontier people more than one hundred years ago. Whoever made up the story was aware that wind is a powerful source of energy that can do a lot of work for people!

Little Charity Simson came running down the street, lickety-split, like a jack rabbit with a coyote on its tail. "Pa! Pa!" she hollered. "There's a wagon comin' into town!"

Her pa, Jack Simson, was standing at the door of his store on Main Street. He looked at her in surprise. "Land sakes, child," he remarked, "that's nothin' to fuss about. Ten or twelve wagons come to town every day."

That was true. It was 1850, and a lot of American folks were traveling west to seek their fortunes. They traveled with all their goods and belongings piled into covered wagons. A covered wagon was like a big, flat box on wheels, with a cloth dome stretched over it. It was pulled by a team of oxen.

As Mr. Simson had said, about a dozen of these wagons came into the town of Westport, Kansas, every day. Westport stood right at the beginning of all the trails that led west—the Santa Fe Trail to New Mexico, the Oregon Trail to the Northwest, and so on. So, all the people heading west had to drive their wagons through Westport.

But little Charity shook her head so hard her braids swung. "This isn't like other wagons, Pa," she said. "There's no oxes pullin' it! *It's movin' by itself!*"

"What?" exclaimed her father. "That's not possible."

But just then he heard a big commotion of dogs barking, horses whinnying, and people shouting. Down the street, followed by an excited crowd, came the wagon that moved by itself.

The wagon looked like an ordinary covered wagon, but with some new parts added to it. A large square platform had been rigged above the cloth cover. A tall mast stuck up from the platform. And on the mast, a big sail billowed in the breeze.

A man was standing on the platform. As the townspeople stared in wonder, he rolled up the sail and let down an anchor on a long rope. The wagon stopped right at Simson's store.

The man dropped a rope ladder and climbed swiftly to the ground. "Howdy, mates," he said to the people who came crowding around. "Smith's the name. Able-Bodied Seaman Smith, formerly of the clipper ship *Sea Sprite.*"

"What in tarnation kind of wagon is that?" exclaimed Mr. Simson. "What makes it go?"

Smith winked at him. "Why, matey, that's a windwagon. The wind makes it go. There's tremendous *power* in wind! It rushes over the sea, pushing big, heavy clipper ships along with ease.

"Since all this prairie land is like a sea—flat, and with wind rushing over it—I sez to myself, why not put a sail on a wagon and let the wind push it over this dry sea?" He winked again. "You know, it costs money to feed oxen, to get ox-power, but the power of the wind is free!"

There were murmurs of appreciation from the crowd. "How fast will it go?" someone asked.

"How fast?" Smith chuckled. "Why, I'll give an ox-drawn wagon a half a day's start and pass it up in an hour!" He looked around at all the people. "But why not see for yourselves? Why don't some of you come aboard for a short cruise? I'll show you what my windwagon can do."

The people looked at one another, uncertainly.

"Let's go, Pa!" begged Charity Simson, pulling at her pa's sleeve.

"All right," agreed Mr. Simson, not wanting to seem fearful in front of his little girl.

"I'll go, too," said Mr. Hawkins, the mayor.

Altogether, seven men and little Charity finally climbed the rope ladder to the deck of

Smith's windwagon. When all were aboard, Smith hoisted the anchor and unfurled the sail. Slowly, the windwagon began to roll up the street as the wind pushed on the sail.

When the wagon got out of town, where there were no buildings to block some of the wind, it started to move faster. A cowboy on a pinto horse had ridden out of town after the wagon, and now the pinto galloped as fast as it could to try to keep up. But it dropped farther and farther back. In a few minutes, horse and rider were only a speck.

"Say, we're really moving, all right," observed Mayor Hawkins, rather nervously.

They certainly were! The wind was pushing the sail so hard that the cloth was stretched into a big bulge. The golden prairie grass flashed past in a blur. The only trouble was that the deck of the windwagon was swaying, just like the deck of a ship at sea. The men, who had been excitedly talking among themselves, grew silent. Some of them began to look rather pale.

The windwagon sped on, with the deck pitching, swaying, and creaking. Charity, who had been chattering happily with Smith, turned to see how her father was enjoying the ride.

"Pa!" she exclaimed. "What's the matter?"

Smith turned to look. Several of the men were hanging feebly over the railing. The others lay weakly on the deck. None of them were pale any longer. They had all turned green.

"Oh-oh," said Smith. Leaning on the rudder
handle, he steered the wagon out of the direct
path of the wind and dropped anchor.
"Lubbers!" he said in disgust. "I sure didn't
think you'd get seasick in the middle of a
Kansas prairie!"

One by one, the men climbed shakily down
the rope ladder. They lay on the ground in a
row. "Take yer cussed windwagon away,
Smith," groaned Mayor Hawkins. "It's all you
say it is—but we never want to see it again!"

Smith shook his head, ruefully. He stooped
to kiss Charity on the cheek. "Goodbye, matey,"
he whispered. "You're the only able-bodied
sailor in the bunch!"

He waited until she scrambled down the
ladder. Then he upped anchor and turned the
wagon so that the wind once again filled the
sail. As Charity watched, the wagon sped
swiftly out of sight over the horizon, pushed
by the mighty energy of the wind.

Putting energy to work

You can water your garden by holding the
hose and spraying the water where you want
it to go. But if you do this, you have to stand
there until the garden is watered. There is
another way—a better way. If you use a
sprinkler, you can get the water to do the
work for you.

Running water is moving. It has kinetic
energy, like other moving things. So while it
sprinkles, it makes the sprinkler turn.

One kind of sprinkler has two bent arms.
As water pushes out through the arms in one
direction, it pushes the arms in the other
direction. The push makes the sprinkler arms
spin, spraying water in a big circle.

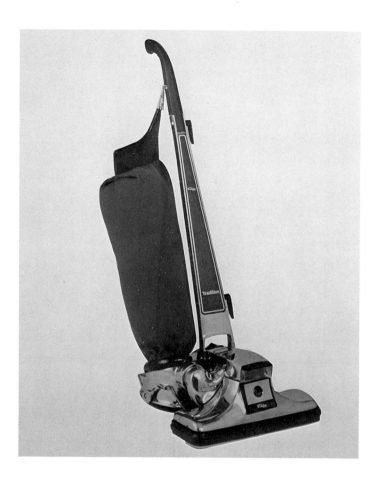

Putting electricity to work

It may look a bit like a dragon, and it may roar like one—but it's really only a vacuum cleaner. And the thing that makes it gobble up dirt from a rug is an electric fan!

When you turn on the vacuum cleaner, you start the fan. The fan blows air into the vacuum cleaner bag. As the air moves into the bag, it leaves an empty space inside the bottom of the vacuum cleaner. An empty space, where there is little air, is called a vacuum. This is what gives the vacuum cleaner its name.

The air outside the vacuum cleaner tries to push into the empty space. But there is only one place where the outside air can get in— through the part that is sweeping the rug. Inside this part of the vacuum cleaner there is a spinning brush. The brush helps to loosen the dirt in the rug. And the rushing air sucks up the dirt and carries it into the bag.

The vacuum cleaner bag is full of tiny holes, so the air easily pushes out through the bag. But the dust doesn't! It gets stuck inside. So the electric "dragon" leaves your rug clean.

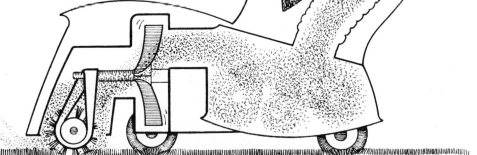

Inside the vacuum cleaner, a fan pulls air (blue) and dust (black) into the bag. The air pushes out through the bag, leaving the dust inside.

Machines
Make It
Easy

Easy as one-two-three

Whirr! The faster you turn the handle, the faster the eggbeater goes. Pretty soon the eggs are a froth of golden-yellow bubbles! The eggbeater makes the work easy—much easier and faster than if you had to stir the eggs with a spoon.

When you mix things with an eggbeater, you are using a machine. An eggbeater isn't very big, it doesn't have very many parts, and it doesn't run by itself. But it does something that all machines do—it helps you do work.

Machines can be any shape and size. But when we think of machines, we usually think of big ones that have a great many parts. The machines we think of are made to do heavy jobs, like washing and drying clothes or mowing lawns.

But some machines are small—even smaller and simpler than an eggbeater. You cut out a picture or snip a string with a small machine—a pair of scissors. You sew with a small machine—a needle. And you tighten a screw with a very simple machine—a screwdriver. The scissors, the needle, and the screwdriver help you the same way bigger machines do—they make a job easier.

A lever is clever

How many times can you lift your best friend higher than your head? How many times can your best friend lift you?

It doesn't sound easy, but it is—and it's fun, too. When you and your friend are on a seesaw, that's exactly what you are doing!

The seesaw you and your friend are riding is really a kind of machine called a lever. A lever makes pushing and lifting easy, even when things are hard to move.

The simplest kind of lever is just a straight stick or board and something to rest it on. Suppose you want to move something

A seesaw is a lever. The rider moving down lifts the other rider into the air.

heavy—for example, a big rock in the corner of your garden. You can push one end of a strong board under the edge of the rock. Then you can rest the middle of the board on a log. This will be the resting place, or fulcrum (FUHL kruhm). The end of the board near you will stick up. Now push down on the high end of the board. The other end will move up—and the heavy rock will move, too.

When you ride a seesaw, you and your friend take turns using it as a lever. The middle of the seesaw is the resting place. Your weight pushes one end down and lifts your friend. Then your friend's weight pushes the other end down and lifts you.

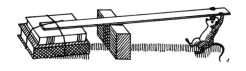

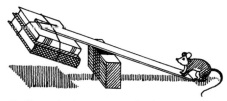

Pulling down one end of the lever (top) lifts the load at the other end (bottom). The brick is the resting place, or fulcrum.

Make an alligator long-arm

Materials

- construction paper
- corrugated cardboard
- glue
- paper fasteners (7)
- pencil
- ruler
- scissors

Levers make it easier to lift big and heavy things. They can also help you pick up things you can't quite reach. This alligator long-arm uses pairs of levers to make other levers move.

Use the ruler to measure six strips of cardboard. Each strip should be about 6½ inches (16.5 centimeters) long and ¾ inch (2 cm) wide. Leave a "tooth" on two of the strips, as shown. Cut out the strips.

Use a pencil to punch holes in the middle of the strips. Fasten pairs of strips together to make three X shapes—two plain shapes and

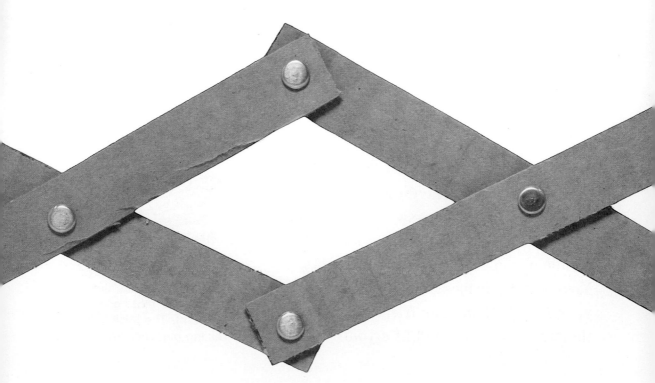

one with teeth. Line up the X shapes as shown and punch the remaining holes. Fasten the shapes together.

Make an alligator head out of construction paper. The head should be almost as long as one of the strips. Then stretch out the long-arm until the teeth on the X touch. Glue the head to the top of the X with teeth, leaving just enough space for the teeth to show. Glue white paper on the teeth to give your alligator a bright smile.

Your alligator long-arm works like a pair of scissors. When you close your end, the end with teeth closes, too. You and your friends can take turns using the long-arm to pick up small cardboard fish or "pirate treasure." See who can make the biggest catch!

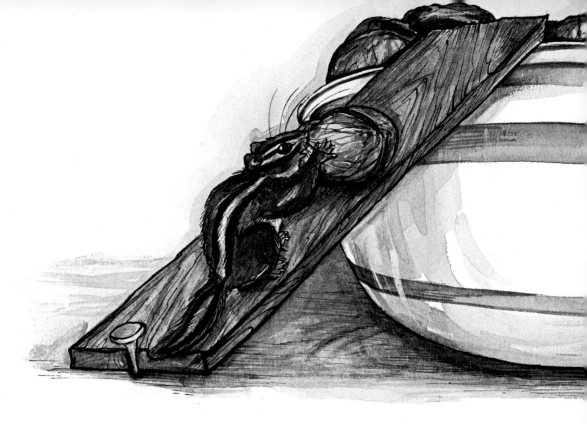

Slides and steps

Is a slanted board a machine? It is if you use it to do some work. It's a kind of simple machine called an inclined plane. *Inclined* means "slanted," and a plane is a flat surface. So an inclined plane is a flat surface that slants, like a slide on a playground.

An inclined plane makes it easy to move things up and down. When you use an inclined plane, you spread out the amount of work you do. If you lift a heavy box onto a table, you move it only a short distance—straight up. But you are doing all the lifting at once. If you slide the box up a slanted board, or inclined plane, you have to move it farther to reach the tabletop. But you do the lifting little by little, so the job is easier.

Inclined planes are a help in moving heavy things. But there are other ways to use them, too. When you wheel your bike up and down a bike ramp, or take a ramp to get on or off an expressway, you are using an inclined plane. And there are ramps at airports and other busy places for people to walk up and down.

The kind of inclined plane you use most often may not look like one. Stairs are an inclined plane! They are not the same smooth shape as a slanted board or a bike ramp, but they help you work in the same way.

When you use stairs, you move on a slant. It's not like climbing a ladder that is straight up and down. The stairs are longer than the ladder would be. But the climb is easier. You lift yourself a little at a time.

A shape that works

Be careful—that knife is sharp! Don't stick yourself with that needle!

Working with sharp things means taking special care. But some things have to be sharp to work well. A dull knife or a needle without a point isn't much help at all.

Sharp things have a special shape that makes work easier. They are really all one kind of machine—a machine called a wedge. The thin, sharp end of a wedge can cut or push into things easily. Then the thicker part of the wedge can push through.

Knives, saws, and scissors are wedges used for cutting. The sharp edge pushes in, and the thicker part spreads the pieces.

Nails and needles are wedges used for pushing into or through things. The point makes it easy for the nail to push into wood or the needle to push through material.

Axes and metal wedges are used to split wood. A chop or a hard hit drives the sharp edge into a log. Then the wider part spreads the wood and makes it split.

Many boats have a wedge-shaped front, or bow. The bow cuts the water and makes it easy for the boat to slide through.

Pounding pushes the thin end of the wedge into the log. Then the thick part splits the wood.

The shape of a screw

Wham! Wham! Wham! All it takes to nail two pieces of wood together is a few strong hits with a hammer. But fastening two pieces of wood together with a screw is a lot harder. The screw has to be turned many times to go into the wood.

A screw has a winding edge called a thread. The thread goes from the end nearly all the way to the top. When you turn the screw, you wind the thread into the wood.

Turning a screw takes more time than pounding a nail the same size. But the winding thread of the screw is much longer than the straight sides of the nail. There is more of it to grip and hold the wood. So for some jobs, a screw works better than a nail. It holds things together more tightly than do nails.

A winding edge

The screw is another simple machine with a special shape. It's really an inclined plane that winds around a center pole. You can easily prove to yourself that the thread of a screw is an inclined plane.

Use a sheet of paper to make a triangle. Fold over the top edge of the paper so that it lines up exactly with the right-hand edge. Cut or tear along the fold, and you will have a triangle. Color the cut edge on both sides of the paper.

The edge that you cut and colored is the inclined plane—it slants. Lay a pencil along one of the other edges of the triangle. Roll the paper around the pencil.

When you look at the rolled-up shape, you will see that the colored edge of the paper turns around and around the pencil. The colored edge of the paper is an inclined plane that winds around a center pole, just like the thread of a screw.

Rolling along

Four wheels, a box, and a handle. That's all a wagon is. But with a wagon you can easily carry a couple of friends or a load of empty bottles—or even give the dog a ride.

When you use a wagon, a simple machine called a wheel and axle is helping you. You can see the wheels—the round parts that roll over the ground. The axles are the rods that connect each pair of wheels. The wheels and axles turn together.

Putting wheels and axles on something makes it easier to move. A wagon without

The wheels and axles on a wagon turn smoothly when you push. You don't have to work very hard to make the wagon move.

wheels would drag over the ground. The scraping, or friction, of the box on the ground would make it hard for you to pull the wagon. But wheels on axles go rolling smoothly along. When wheels and axles are used, even big loads can be moved without much friction.

Cars, trucks, and buses are some big machines that have wheel-and-axle parts. Those parts work just like the wheels and axles on a wagon. The only difference is that a car, truck, or bus has an engine that does the pushing. When you use a wagon, *you* do the pushing or pulling.

Turn, turn, turn

How many wheels do you use in a day?

You can count wheels that roll—bicycle wheels, car wheels, and bus wheels, too. They help you get places. A push from you or an engine makes the axle turn. And the axle makes the wheels go around. The wheels are much bigger around than the axle, so they roll a long way each time the axle turns. The wheels help to get a lot of speed and distance from each turn of the axle.

But you can count other kinds of wheels, too—wheels that don't roll. These wheels help you to do other kinds of work. A doorknob is a kind of wheel-and-axle machine. The knob is the wheel! You turn it to make the axle pull back the latch so the door can open.

A pencil sharpener has a wheel and axle, too. The handle may not look much like a wheel, but it really is part of one. When you turn the handle, it turns an axle that makes the other parts work.

A doorknob, a pencil sharpener, a can opener, and many other things with handles that turn, all work in the same way. When you use these machines, you are turning a wheel to make an axle move. The axle doesn't move fast or far, but it helps you get a lot of work from each turn of the wheel.

What am I?

The answers to all of these riddles are wheel-and-axle machines. Can you find two that roll and two that turn?

1. My axles are two, but my wheels are three.
   Even little kids ride on me.
   What am I?

2. I'm part of a car, but I never roll.
   You turn me the way the car should go.
   What am I?

3. My wheels are four and I'm in a store.
   If you push me around, you can carry more.
   What am I?

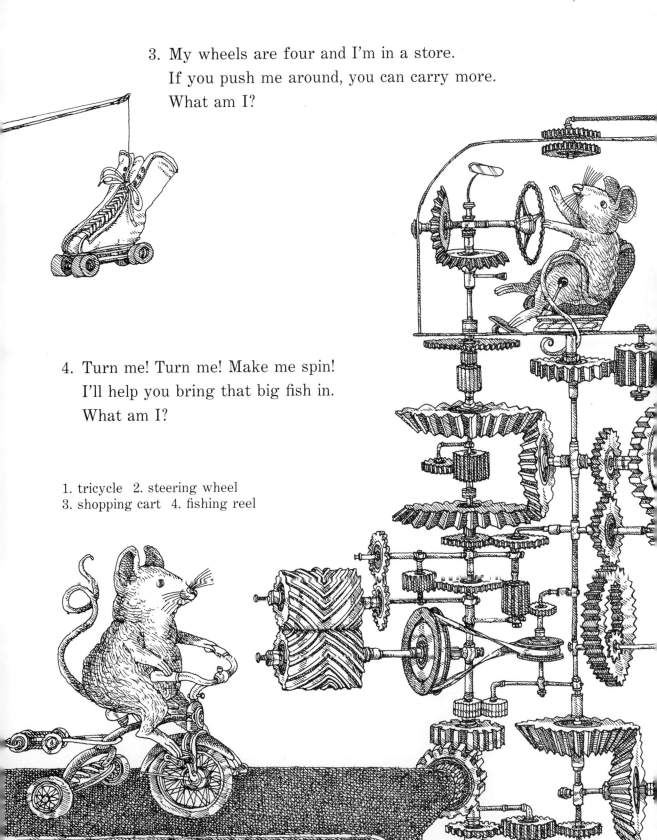

4. Turn me! Turn me! Make me spin!
   I'll help you bring that big fish in.
   What am I?

1. tricycle 2. steering wheel
3. shopping cart 4. fishing reel

Ups and downs

Suppose someone asked you to lift a hippopotamus out of its hippopotamus-sized bathtub! It sounds impossible—but with a simple machine called a pulley, you could do it!

A pulley is a special kind of wheel and axle. The rim of the wheel is grooved so that a rope or steel cable can fit around it. When one end of the rope is pulled down, the rope slides over the wheel, which turns on the axle. Then the load at the other end moves up.

With one pulley, the load moves up as far as you pull the rope down. You work just as hard to pull the rope as you would to pick up

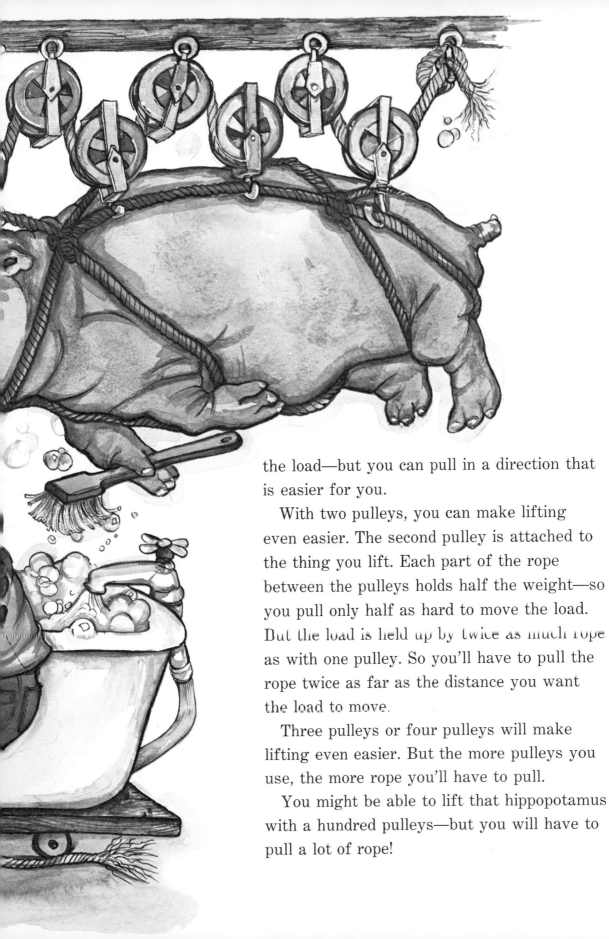

the load—but you can pull in a direction that is easier for you.

With two pulleys, you can make lifting even easier. The second pulley is attached to the thing you lift. Each part of the rope between the pulleys holds half the weight—so you pull only half as hard to move the load. But the load is held up by twice as much rope as with one pulley. So you'll have to pull the rope twice as far as the distance you want the load to move.

Three pulleys or four pulleys will make lifting even easier. But the more pulleys you use, the more rope you'll have to pull.

You might be able to lift that hippopotamus with a hundred pulleys—but you will have to pull a lot of rope!

The Swiss Family Robinson

The Swiss Family Robinson tells of the adventures of a family that is shipwrecked on an uninhabited island. The story was made up more than 180 years ago by a real Swiss family. They imagined they were shipwrecked, then thought of all the things they would have to do to stay alive and make themselves comfortable.

The Wyss family knew that understanding how to use tools, how machines work, and how things can be made would be most important. So, in the story, the father keeps everyone safe and comfortable through his knowledge of such simple machines as the lever, the wheel, the pulley, and the screw.

For seven days, the ship on which the family is sailing is caught in a terrible storm. Then it is blown onto the rocks near an island. The crew abandons the ship, taking all the boats and leaving the family behind.

The storm comes to an end, but the ship is slowly breaking apart. Determined to save his family, the father builds a boat that can carry them all to the island. The story is told by the father.

The Tree House

by Johann Wyss

We soon found four large casks, made of
sound wood and strongly bound with iron
hoops. These were floating with other things
in the water in the hold. We managed to fish
them out and drag them to a suitable place
for launching them. They were exactly what I
wanted. It was hard work, but I succeeded in
sawing them in half.

I next found a long, thin plank on which I
fastened my tubs. The two ends of this I bent
upward so as to form a keel. Two other
planks were nailed along the sides of the tubs
and brought to a point at each end. All was
firmly secured and nailed together.

When we thought all was ready for the
launch, we found, to our dismay, that it was
so heavy and clumsy that even our united
efforts could not move it an inch.

"I must have a lever," cried I. "Run and
fetch the capstan bar."

Fritz quickly brought one. Earlier, I had
made some rollers by cutting up a long spar.
As I raised the forepart of my boat with the
bar, my sons placed a roller under it.

"How is it, Father," inquired Ernest, "that
with that thing you alone can do more than
all of us together?"

I explained, as well as I could in a hurry,

the principle of the lever. I promised to have
a long talk on the subject of Mechanics,
should we have a future opportunity.

Placing a second and third roller under the
boat, we once more began to push, this time
with success. Soon our gallant craft was safely
launched. But, alas, she leaned to one side. Some
heavy things being thrown in, however, the boat
righted itself by degrees.

But it was plain that something more was
required. So, to make her perfectly safe, I made
outriggers to keep the balance. I did this by
nailing long poles across at the stem and stern,
and fixing empty brandy casks at the ends of
each pole.

By this time it was too late to attempt the voyage, so we sat down to enjoy a comfortable supper. Then retiring to our berths, peaceful sleep prepared us all for the exertions of the coming day.

> Launching the boat by means of the lever and rollers (wheels), the family makes its way to the island. Some of the animals on the ship—two dogs, goats, a cow, and a donkey—manage to get to the island by swimming. And, in time, a lot of wood from the broken-up ship floats to shore.
> For a time, the family lives in a cave. Then the mother discovers a grove of huge trees. She persuades her husband to try building a tree house.

The wonderful appearance of the enormous trees, and the calm beauty of the spot, fully

came up to the enthusiastic description my wife had given me. And she gladly heard me say that if I could build a house among the branches, it would be the safest and most charming home in the world.

"What sort of a tree do you suppose this to be, Father?" inquired Ernest. "Is not the leaf something like a walnut?"

"There is a resemblance, but in my opinion these gigantic trees must be mangroves or wild figs. I have heard their enormous height described, and also the arching roots supporting the main trunk."

We examined the different trees, and chose one which seemed most suited to our purpose. The branches spread at a great height above us. It was my intention to construct a rope ladder, if we could succeed in getting a string across a strong bough.

My sons fastened together some long reeds and tried to measure the height of the lowest branch. They soon found they could not touch the branch.

"Hullo, my boys," I said, when I discovered what they were about, "that is not the way to set to work. Geometry will simplify the operation considerably. With its help, the altitudes of the highest mountains are ascertained. We may, therefore, easily find the height of the branch."

So saying, I soon worked out the height and announced that we should henceforth live thirty feet above the ground. This I wanted to know, that I might make a rope ladder of the necessary length.

Taking some reeds, I made half a dozen arrows. I then took a strong bamboo, bent it, and strung it so as to form a bow.

"Elizabeth," I said, to my wife, "can you supply me with a ball of stout thread?"

"Certainly," replied she.

I fastened one end of the thread to one of my arrows and aimed at a large branch above me. The arrow flew up, carried the thread over the branch, and fell at our feet. Thus was the first step accomplished. Now for the rope ladder!

Fritz had obtained two coils of rope, each about forty feet in length. We stretched these on the ground side by side. Then Fritz cut some bamboo rods into two-foot lengths for the steps. As he handed them to me, I passed them through knots I had prepared in the ropes. Jack fastened each end with a nail driven through the wood.

When the ladder was finished, I tied a length of cord to one end of the thread and pulled the cord over the bough. I then used the cord to pull the ladder up. This done, I fixed the lower end of the ladder firmly to the ground by means of stakes and all was ready for an ascent. The boys, who had been watching me with intense interest, were each eager to be first.

"Jack shall have the honor," said I, "as he

is the lightest. Up with you, my boy, and do not break your neck."

Jack, active as a monkey, sprang up the ladder and quickly gained the top.

"Three cheers for the nest!" he shouted, waving his cap. "Hurrah, hurrah, hurrah for our jolly nest! What a grand house we will have up here. Come along, Fritz!"

His brother was soon by his side, and with a hammer and nails fastened the ladder securely. I followed and looked around. The tree was just right for our purpose. The branches were very strong and so closely interwoven that no beams would be needed to support the floor.

I now called for a pulley. My wife fastened one to the cord hanging beside the ladder and I hauled it up. I then fastened the pulley to a stout branch above me. It would be used when we hauled up the beams the next day. I then made other preparations, that there might be no delay on the morrow.

Early next morning we were astir and went about our various occupations. My wife milked the goats and cow, while we gave the animals their food. Afterward, we went down to the beach to collect more wood for our building operations. To the larger beams we harnessed the cow and ass, while we dragged the rest.

Fritz and I then ascended the tree and finished the preparations I had begun the night before. All useless boughs we lopped off, leaving a few about six feet from the floor. From these we would sling our hammocks. Other branches, still higher, would support a temporary roof of sailcloth.

My wife fastened the planks to a rope passed through the pulley I had fixed to the bough. By this means, Fritz and I hauled the planks up. These we arranged side by side on the boughs, so as to form a smooth, solid floor. Round this platform I built a wall of planks. Then, throwing the sailcloth over the higher branches, we drew it down and firmly nailed it to the wall.

Our house was thus enclosed on three sides, for the trunk protected us from behind. The front was left open to admit the fresh sea breeze. We then hauled up our hammocks and bedding and slung them from the branches we had left for that purpose.

We then descended from the tree and my wife prepared supper. After eating, we lit our watch fire. Leaving the dogs on guard below, we ascended the ladder. Fritz, Ernest, and Jack were up in a moment. Their mother followed very cautiously. When she was safely up, I took little Franz on my back. I let go the fastenings which held the lower end of the ladder to the ground. Swinging to and fro, I slowly ascended.

Then for the first time we were all together in our new home. I drew up the ladder. With a great sense of security, I offered up our evening prayer and we retired for the night.

> Thus, with little more than such simple machines as a pulley and nails (wedges), father and sons build the tree house. When the mother finds it difficult to use the rope ladder to climb up and down, her husband puts to use his knowledge of another simple machine—the screw—and builds a spiral staircase inside the tree trunk.

A door first had to be made. At the base of the trunk we cut away the bark and formed an opening just the size of the door we had brought from the captain's cabin. This door, hinges and all, was ready to hang.

The clearing of the dead wood from the

center of the trunk occupied us some time. At length, we had the satisfaction of seeing this done. Then, as we stood below, we could look up the trunk, which was like a great smooth funnel, and see the sky above. It was now ready for the staircase.

First, we erected in the center a stout sapling to form an axis around which to build the spiral. We cut notches in this to receive the steps, and notches in the tree to support the outer ends of the steps. The steps themselves we formed carefully and neatly of planks from the wreck. We then nailed them firmly in place. Upward and upward we built. As we went, we cut windows in the trunk to admit light and air.

When we were flush with the top of the center pole, we erected another pole to reach to the top of the tree. Fastening it firmly, we built in the same way round it until we reached the floor of our nest.

To make it easy to climb the stairs, we ran a handrail on each side. One rail went round the center pole and the other followed the curve of the trunk.

The tree house completed, the family makes itself safe and comfortable. They have many exciting adventures on the island. Are they rescued? Read the book and find out!

Wheels with teeth

Why should a wheel have teeth? Wheels don't eat! But some wheels use teeth to get a lot of work done—and they can do things that other wheels can't do.

A wheel with teeth is called a gear. It's a wheel that makes other wheels move. If you look at an eggbeater, you can see three gears. The big one with the handle is the gear you turn. The teeth on this gear fit into the spaces between the teeth on the two small gears. When you turn the handle, the teeth on the big gear push the teeth of the small gears and make these gears turn.

Finding out about gears

What special things can gears do? Here is a project that will help you find out.

Cut three strips of paper long enough to go around the lids. The strips should be ¾ inch (2 centimeters) wide. Glue one strip around each lid.

Mark an arrow on each lid, as shown. Push a pin through the center of each lid.

Materials

- cardboard box
- corrugated packing paper
- marker
- pins (3 long)
- plastic lids (1 small, 2 large)
- white glue

Which way?

Put the two big gears on the box. Point the arrows in the same direction. Fit the teeth together. Push the pins into the box. What happens when you turn one gear?

The second gear moves in the opposite direction. It always turns the other way.

Left, right, left

Make a chain of three gears. Turn the first one. What happens to the other gears?

The first gear makes the second gear turn the opposite way. And the second gear makes the third gear turn the same way as the first gear.

Around and around

Put the two big gears on the box, with both arrows pointing in the same direction. Turn one gear around exactly once. How far does it make the other gear turn? How fast does it make the gear move?

Now use a big gear and a small gear. Turn the big gear once. How far and how fast does it make the small gear turn? What happens if you turn the small gear once?

When two gears are the same size, both gears turn at the same speed. When a big gear turns a small gear, the small gear turns faster. And when a small gear turns a big gear, the big gear moves more slowly.

Machines from machines

It's easy to see how a pair of scissors works. Every time you squeeze the handles together, the blades cut into the paper.

Using a pair of scissors is simple—but scissors are not a simple machine. They are really two kinds of simple machines put together. Each half of the scissors is a lever. And the blade on each half is a wedge.

Most of the machines we use every day are made up of two or more simple machines put together. In fact, a list of what goes into most machines would look like an addition problem in arithmetic.

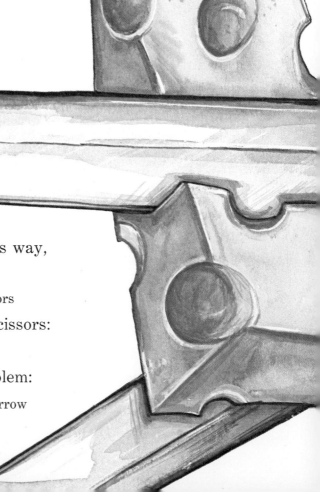

If you think of a pair of scissors this way, here's what you get:

lever + wedge + lever + wedge = scissors

A knife is more like half a pair of scissors:

lever + wedge = knife

A wheelbarrow is another easy problem:

lever + lever + wheel and axle — wheelbarrow

A revolving door gets to be a much longer addition problem, but it is made up of the same simple machines:

wheel and axle + lever + lever + lever + lever = revolving door

Listing all the simple machines in something as complicated as a typewriter would be an addition problem pages and pages long! But if you wrote out the problem, there would still be only six kinds of things—six simple machines—to add together. Your list would be made up of levers, inclined planes, wedges, screws, pulleys, and wheels and axles.

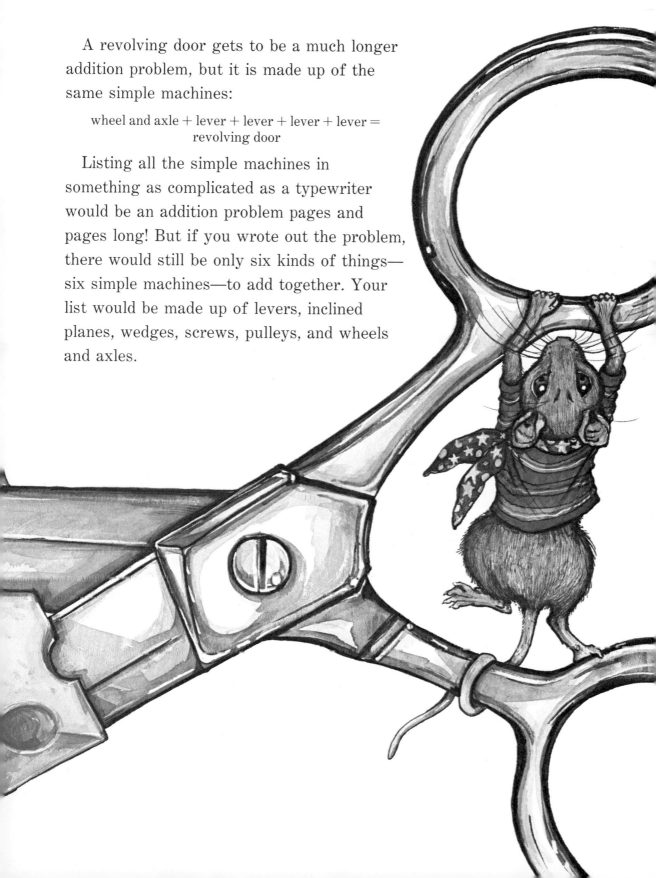

The moving stairs

Hump, the Escalator slid
Out of the basement—yes, he did!
Out of the basement unawares,
Flattened a moment, then made a stairs;
Made a stairs that moved and crawled
Up through a runway, narrow-walled.

Here I stood on the floor below,
Then on a stair-step rising slow.
Over the heads of the shoppers then—
Dressed-up ladies and bothered men;

An escalator that carries you from one floor to
another in a busy department store is a moving
inclined plane—an inclined plane on wheels. The
wheels are out of sight, under the steps.

Over the aisles of hats and hose—
Over the shelf displays I rose!
Suddenly stood on the second floor,
Not on a stairway any more.

Every rider ahead of me
Took it stiffly and solemnly.
Nobody paid a penny's fare—
Or knew they had ridden a Magic Stair!

Hump, the Escalator
by Dorothy Faubion

Putting machines to work

Turn the key at the back of the alarm clock once . . . twice . . . three times. At first the key turns easily. But as you keep winding, the key turns harder and harder. Finally the clock is wound as far as it will go.

When you wind the clock, you turn a spring inside and make it coil up tight. You give the coiled spring potential energy—stored-up energy that will make the parts move.

The wound-up spring begins to uncoil a little at a time. Its energy is used to turn a set of gears that move at different speeds. The gear for the minute hand turns all the way around once every hour. The gear for the hour hand moves much more slowly. It takes twelve hours to make a single turn.

There is enough energy stored in the spring to keep the gears moving and the clock hands turning for a whole day. At the end of the day, the spring is uncoiled and loose. Then you wind it again—to store up more energy to keep the clock running.

A wind-up clock runs on the energy stored in a tightly coiled spring (left). As the spring unwinds, the clock ticks away. When the spring is completely unwound (right), the clock stops.

What's the Matter?

"Something" for everyone

What's in the package? You won't know for sure until you open it—but it's fun to guess. You can tell about how big the present inside the wrapping paper is. And you can tell about how heavy it is when you lift the package.

The package and the present inside it are made up of something—something that has weight and takes up space. That "something" is called *matter* (MAT uhr).

Anything that has weight and takes up space is matter—so *you* are matter, too. And so is a rock, a dandelion, a rabbit, or a puddle of water. There is matter in everything around you.

Even the air you breathe is matter. You don't really feel how much air weighs, because most things are heavier than air. But air does have weight. And it takes up space. You can feel it take up space when you breathe in. And you can see it take up space when you blow up a balloon.

What's the Matter?

What's the matter, do you ask?
I'll tell you right away.
It's *everything* around you, as
you work, or sleep, or play.

A chair is matter, a table, too,
and so is a rock or tree.
A cloud, a star, a blade of grass,
a raindrop, a bumblebee.

The earth is matter, so is the sea,
and the sky is matter, too.
(Of course what matters most of all
is the matter that is *you!*)

There's matter almost everywhere,
except in one special place—
the vast, black, lonely *emptiness*,
that we call outer space.

Tom McGowen

Bits and pieces

What's in a sand castle? Millions and millions of tiny grains of sand. The *many* grains of sand are packed together to make a *single* shape—a castle with towers, walls, and bridges.

And what are you made of? Millions and millions of tiny bits, each one even smaller than a grain of sand! You and all the other things around you—people and cars, rocks, water, and even the air—are made of bits that are put together in different ways.

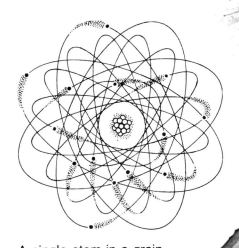

A single atom in a grain of sand is too small to see. But its parts might be arranged like this. Tiny electrons speed around the center, or nucleus, which is made of larger bits.

These bits are called *atoms* (AT uhmz). Atoms are much smaller than a grain of sand. In fact, they are too small for you to see. But if you could see them, you would find that these tiny atoms are made up of even smaller pieces!

Every atom has a center part called a *nucleus* (NOO klee uhs). And outside the nucleus there are even tinier bits called *electrons* (ih LEHK trahnz).

Even though atoms are so tiny you can't see them, they still have weight and take up space. They are tiny bits of matter. Everything that is matter—even you—is made up of these tiny bits.

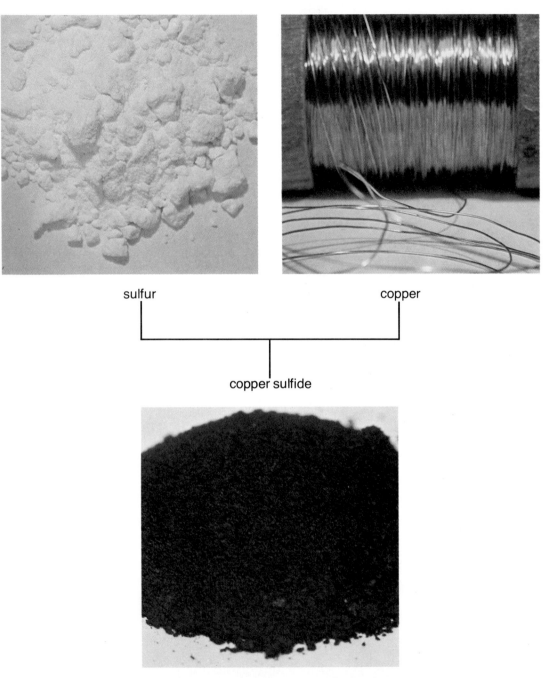

sulfur   copper

copper sulfide

Sulfur is a soft, yellow element and copper is a shiny, red-brown element. But when copper atoms and sulfur atoms join together, they form a different kind of material—a black, powdery compound called copper sulfide.

Kinds of matter

How many kinds of matter are there? So many that if you started to count them, you probably would never finish!

But if you could sort out the atoms in all of that matter, you would find that there are only about a hundred kinds. Each of the hundred kinds of atoms has a nucleus, or center, of a different size, and a different number of electrons.

Some kinds of matter are made up of only one kind of atom. These kinds of matter are called *elements* (EHL uh muhnts). Gold is an element—a piece of pure gold is made up of just gold atoms. Iron is an element, too—it is made up of just iron atoms.

But most kinds of matter are made of different kinds of atoms joined together. These kinds of matter are called *compounds* (KAHM powndz).

Water is made of an element called oxygen (AHK suh juhn) and an element called hydrogen (HY druh juhn). By itself oxygen is an invisible gas—you can't see it. So is hydrogen. But when they join, they make a liquid you can see, feel, and pour—water.

Compounds can have many more kinds of atoms. And the atoms can be put together in different ways. But all compounds are made from two or more of the hundred or so kinds of atoms we know.

Building blocks

Atoms are the "building blocks" of matter. They fit together to make all the things there are. Most kinds of matter are made of atoms that are joined together. These groups of joined atoms are called *molecules* (MAHL uh kyoolz).

Molecules can be very simple. When you breathe air, your body takes in molecules of a gas called oxygen. Each oxygen molecule is simply two oxygen atoms joined together.

But molecules can be complicated, too. The "vinegary" taste in vinegar comes from a molecule containing two carbon atoms, four hydrogen atoms, and two oxygen atoms. And some molecules are made of thousands of atoms! Bread and potatoes contain giant molecules that look like chains—chains up to forty thousand atoms long.

When two atoms of hydrogen (H) and one atom of oxygen (O) are joined, they form a single molecule of water.

The sour taste of vinegar comes from molecules made of carbon, hydrogen, and oxygen. Each molecule contains two carbon atoms (C), four hydrogen atoms (H), and two oxygen atoms (O). The atoms in each molecule are joined together in exactly the same way.

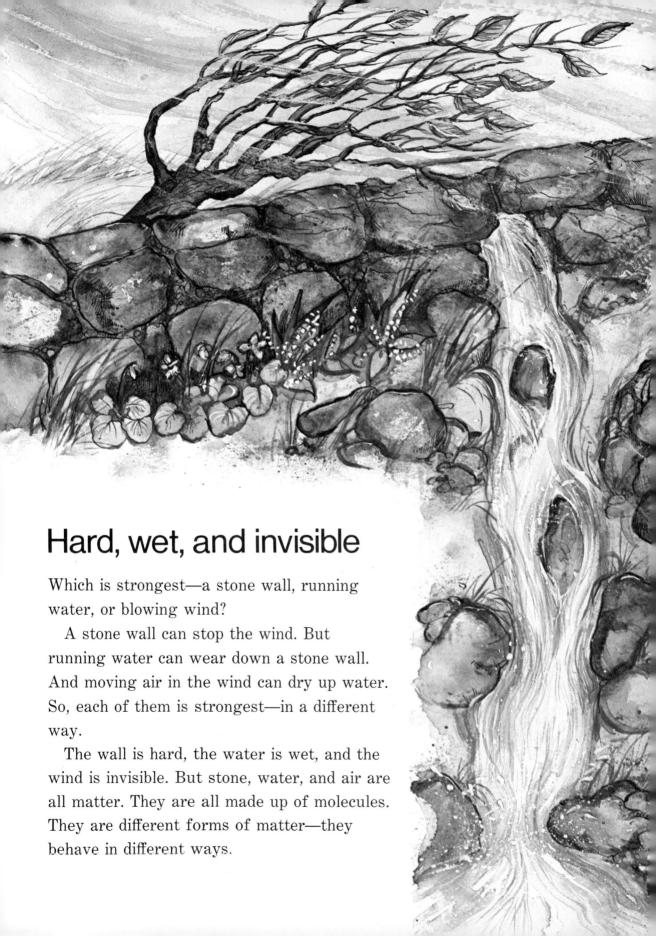

Hard, wet, and invisible

Which is strongest—a stone wall, running water, or blowing wind?

A stone wall can stop the wind. But running water can wear down a stone wall. And moving air in the wind can dry up water. So, each of them is strongest—in a different way.

The wall is hard, the water is wet, and the wind is invisible. But stone, water, and air are all matter. They are all made up of molecules. They are different forms of matter—they behave in different ways.

Stone is a *solid* (SAHL ihd)—it has a shape of its own. The molecules in solids are very close together. They pull hard on each other—much as magnets do. This pull makes solids keep their shape.

Water is a *liquid* (LIHK wihd)—it has no shape of its own. Molecules in a liquid are farther apart than in a solid—they don't pull as hard on each other. So the molecules of a liquid can slide around. That's why liquids have no shape.

And air is a *gas*. It has no shape of its own, either. Its molecules are so far apart that they hardly pull on each other at all. Molecules of a gas bounce around so easily that they can squeeze into a balloon or spread out to fill a room.

All the kinds of matter around us are solids or liquids or gases. So in everything around us, molecules behave in certain ways. They hang together tightly, slide around each other, or move about freely in space.

Dear Mom and Dad,
we have arrived safely—
and we're hungry!
We're already learning to
cook Earth-style meals.
Here are some things
we've fixed!

Solid, liquid, gas

Tikka and her brother Ronk are two of the
first Space Scouts ever to visit Earth. They
haven't yet learned the names for Earth
foods.

Here is part of their first letter home. See
if you can guess what foods they have eaten.
If you aren't sure, you'll find the answers
listed on the next page.

Breakfast

1. We melted a can of cold solid, stirred it
   with a liquid, and drank some.
2. We heated slices of a solid until they
   turned crisp. Then we spread them with a
   solid that melted.
3. We opened two white solids filled with
   soft, gooey liquid. We mixed the liquid and
   heated it in a pan until it turned to a soft
   yellow solid.

Lunch

4. We heated a liquid that was filled with chunks of solids.

5. We heated two slices of a solid with another solid between them. The middle solid melted.

6. We drank a cold liquid filled with tiny bubbles of a gas.

Dinner

7. We cooked thin sticks of a solid. When the sticks were soft, we poured hot, red liquid on them.

8. We tossed raw solids and then poured on a bit of liquid.

9. We scooped a frozen solid out of a box.

Earth foods

2. hot buttered toast
7. spaghetti with tomato sauce
6. soda pop
1. frozen orange juice
8. tossed salad
3. scrambled eggs
4. vegetable soup
9. ice cream
5. toasted cheese sandwich

Speeding up molecules

Can you fry ice cubes? You can try—but if you heat ice cubes in a pan, they won't be ice cubes any more. The ice will melt into water. And, after a while, the water will boil and turn into steam. What makes the ice cubes change?

Ice melts because something happens to its molecules. Heat energy makes the molecules move faster. As the molecules speed up, they begin to move away from each other. Then the ice becomes a liquid—water.

Heat speeds up the molecules in liquids, too. So, as the molecules speed up, they move even farther apart. Finally they lose almost all their pull on each other. Then the liquid evaporates (ih VAP uh rayts). It becomes a gas.

And that's what happens when water boils. Heat makes the molecules roll and tumble faster and faster in the pan. When the water molecules are moving fast enough, they become steam—they evaporate and mix with the molecules in the air.

Heat changes ice cubes from a solid (ice) to a liquid (water), and then to a gas (steam).

Slowing down molecules

In stormy weather, raindrops trickle down the outside of the window. But sometimes, in very cool weather, the *inside* of the window is cloudy and wet. Where does the film of water on the inside of the window come from?

The cloudy film of water comes from water vapor (VAY puhr)—water molecules mixed with the air inside the house. The water collects on the windows when the glass is cool.

Water vapor is a gas. The molecules of water vapor are as warm as the air around them in the house, so they move very fast. But when the molecules hit the cool glass in the window, they lose heat. As the molecules grow cooler, they slow down and move closer together. When they are moving slowly enough, they condense (kuhn DEHNS), or turn into tiny drops of liquid.

Sometimes, when the weather is very cold, the glass in the window gets much colder than the air inside the house. Then the molecules of water vapor lose even more heat when they touch the glass. They slow down much more and move much closer together. When they get close enough to pull hard on each other, they freeze. Then the window is covered with frost—thin, feathery bits of solid ice.

Making changes

You can change matter from one form to another by making molecules speed up and slow down. This project will show you how.

A melting race

Make sure the glasses are at room temperature. Put an ice cube in the first glass, a small piece of butter in the second glass, and a penny in the third glass. Leave the glasses for five minutes. Which things have melted?

At room temperature, some of the ice cube melts. The butter softens, but it doesn't melt. The penny doesn't change.

Next, pour one inch (2.5 centimeters) of hot water into the pan. Set the glasses in the pan and leave them for five minutes. What changes do you see?

The hot water makes the molecules speed up. Much more of the ice cube melts. The butter melts, too. But the molecules in the penny don't speed up much—it doesn't melt.

Materials

- butter (cold)
- glasses (3, same size)
- ice cubes (2)
- jar lid (metal)
- pan
- penny
- water

Liquid to gas to liquid

Fill one glass half full with hot water. Set the jar lid on the glass, upside down. Then place an ice cube in the lid. After five minutes, remove the ice cube. Carefully lift the lid. What do you see on the side that covered the glass?

There are drops of water on the lid. Some molecules in the hot water changed to gas. But when the molecules of gas hit the cold lid, they slowed down. They condensed and became a liquid again.

The Signal in the Rock

Elements are the simplest kind of matter, with only a single kind of atom. They are the building blocks for all other matter.

But which kinds of matter are elements? How many elements are there? So far, scientists have discovered more than a hundred elements. A few elements have been known since ancient times. But others have remained "hidden" for years, mixed with other kinds of matter.

Marie Sklodowska Curie was a young scientist, still studying at a university, when she spotted a clue to what she thought might be one of these "hidden" elements. She and her husband Pierre began a search for this element—a longer, harder search than either of them ever dreamed it would be.

Marie shivered as she walked homeward through the Paris streets. But she hardly noticed the damp winter wind—she had gotten so used to her tiny, chilly laboratory that the weather outside didn't seem cold any more.

Besides, her mind was somewhere else. The experiment she had finished and written up that day—February 6, 1898—was one that she had done a dozen times. Each time, she had gotten the same result—and she couldn't explain it.

The rock Marie was working with gave off rays of energy. Marie knew about an unusual element called uranium that gave off such rays of energy. And she had studied one other element, thorium, that gave off the same mysterious rays.

These rays were like a signal. Marie knew that if a rock gave off such rays, it contained uranium or thorium. But the "signal" from the rock she had just measured made no sense at all. The rock gave off *stronger* rays than either uranium or thorium. In fact, the rays were stronger than uranium and thorium rays together!

She was still thinking about the experiment when she got home. "Something is wrong," she told her husband Pierre. "Maybe I'm making the same mistake over and over again.

Or maybe the instruments don't work properly in such a cold room. Or—Pierre, do you suppose the rock contains something we don't know about?"

"A new element?" he asked.

"Yes," she said, "a new element."

The longer they talked, the more certain Marie felt. There *had* to be a new element in the rock—a kind of matter no one had yet discovered. But if there was a new element, there couldn't be much of it. Other scientists had studied rocks of this kind, and they hadn't found it. And the new element must be very powerful if such a tiny bit of it gave off such tremendous amounts of energy. It was worth looking for.

Both Curies set to work. Their first task was to find a kind of matter in which the "signal" was especially strong. After testing several minerals, they chose a rock called pitchblende for their experiments. Pitchblende contained uranium—but it gave off rays that were four times as strong as uranium rays!

Marie and Pierre treated the pitchblende with chemicals to break the different kinds of molecules apart. Each broken-down part was tested to see if it gave off the powerful rays. If it didn't, they got rid of it. But if it did give off energy, they went to work again, trying to break that part of the pitchblende into even smaller parts.

There *was* a new element in pitchblende—in

fact, there were two! Two of the broken-down parts gave "signals"—the rays the Curies were looking for. By July, 1898, the Curies knew enough about one of the elements to announce what they had found. Because Marie was from Poland, they named the element *polonium.*

But there was a problem with the other new element. It was still in hiding. The amount of it in pitchblende was amazingly small. To make even a tiny bit of the element, Marie and Pierre would have to treat tons of rock!

Pitchblende is very valuable because of the uranium it contains. The Curies couldn't hope to buy much of it. But after the uranium was removed, the leftover pitchblende dust was thrown away. Maybe they could buy the dust.

With a friend's help, they located a mining company. Everything was soon arranged. They could have the dust—tons of it! But they would have to pay to have it shipped. And they would have to find a place to put it—a place bigger than the tiny, damp laboratory Marie had been using.

At the Sorbonne, the university where Marie studied, there was not even a spare corner. But Pierre found an old wooden shed with a glass roof at the School of Physics, where he worked.

The shed was big enough, but it wasn't really what they needed. The glass roof would make the shed hot as an oven in the summer sun.

And the cracked and broken panes would leak
whenever it snowed or rained. The floor was
dirt, covered with tar. The battered iron stove
was too small to heat the room. And there was
no chemical equipment anywhere!

"Well, it will have to do," Marie said. "We
must make the best of it."

So, when the heavy horse-drawn wagons
pulled up to the School of Physics, there was
a place to put the sacks of pitchblende dust.

Marie and Pierre ran into the street to watch
the sacks unloaded. Marie ripped one of them
open so she could see the powdery brown stuff
in which the mysterious element was hiding.
It was there somewhere—the element they had
already named *radium*. All they had to do
was get it out!

All of the pitchblende had to be broken
down with chemicals. Then the parts had to
be broken down again—and again—and
again, until the strange new element was
found.

Sack by sack, Marie began treating the
brown dust—mixing it with other compounds,
boiling it, pouring liquids from one huge jar
to another. It was dangerous to work inside
the shed with so many strong chemicals. So
in all but the worst weather, Marie boiled her
dust outside. Day after day she stood in the
courtyard over the huge kettles, stirring the
bubbling mud with an iron rod as tall as she
was.

The work was hard, and she and Pierre
were tired. The amount of pitchblende that
had to be treated was enormous. Every few
months more sacks of brown dust arrived,
and Marie began all over again.

But they were making progress! The tests
she and Pierre made on the broken-up, boiled-
down remains of the pitchblende showed that
the "signals"—the rays from the mysterious
element—were growing stronger and

stronger. Each step in the treatment took away some of the matter that did not contain the element. So what was left had more and more radium in it.

Now Marie no longer needed to stand outdoors. The material had been broken up and boiled down so much that it was very concentrated—there was much less of it. So it could be kept in the shed, in jars.

But time and time again, Marie's careful work and Pierre's delicate measurements were spoiled—by the heat in summer, by the cold in winter, by the wind at any time of year. Sometimes, when Marie had made an almost-pure material, the wind whistling in through the cracked glass roof dumped bits of iron or coal dust into it. Then she would have to do the work again.

But they were so close, Marie couldn't give up. "Pierre," she said, "what do you think radium will look like?"

Pierre thought a moment. "I don't know," he said softly. "I would like it to have a beautiful color."

And then they had it—radium. From all the tons of pitchblende dust, Marie was able to prepare one-tenth of a gram of material that was mostly radium—a little more than three-*thousandths* of an ounce. It had taken nearly four years of stirring and boiling, treating and testing, and beginning again. But radium was no longer an idea. The crystals in their tiny glass jars were real. They were a kind of matter no one had ever seen before.

Now that Marie and Pierre had found this strange element, they couldn't bear to leave it alone. Late that night, they had to go back to the old shed for one more look. They walked across the courtyard behind the School of Physics and unlocked the door.

"Pierre," Marie said, "don't light the lamp. Look!"

Inside the shed, they could see their radium. The new element had something better than a beautiful color. It had so much energy that it glowed! In the dark, the little glass containers were like tiny blue fireflies!

There was still a great deal to be learned about radium—so much work to do! But for the moment, Marie was satisfied. The shining new element was there, just as she had said it would be.

Marie and Pierre Curie won some of the highest awards in science for their discovery of radium and their study of radioactivity— the way atoms behave when they produce the strong, high-energy rays.

But Marie Curie's work did not stop there. She spent the rest of her life working with radium and with other radioactive elements. Before her death in 1934, she saw the rays used to save lives—to treat diseases which had never before been cured.

The search for new kinds of matter is still going on. Scientists have found new ways to explore the invisible world inside molecules and atoms. They have even found ways to *make* new elements.

Matter forever!

After a log burns in a fireplace, only a few handfuls of soft ashes are left. Most of the matter in the log seems to be gone. But is it really gone? No! It has simply changed into other kinds of matter.

Wood is made up of molecules, like all other matter. So, when the wood burns, the heat makes the molecules speed up and begin to break apart.

Most of the atoms from the broken-up molecules combine themselves into different kinds of matter. Some atoms form molecules of gases that escape into the air. Other atoms

form molecules of water—but because the water is very hot, it quickly becomes a gas and escapes, too. A few atoms don't get quite hot enough to form molecules of gas. They are carried off as smoke.

Some kinds of molecules in the log just don't burn—the heat doesn't break them apart. Those molecules are easy to find! They are the ashes left when the rest of the wood has burned.

Any kind of matter can be broken up and rearranged into other kinds of matter. But when this happens, the atoms and molecules in the matter don't really get used up. They are still around, if you know where to look!

How does a gasoline engine work?

When a gasoline engine runs, matter is changed from one form to another, and energy is released.

Liquid gasoline flows through a pipe from the tank to the engine. On the way, it passes through a special part that scoops in air. The fast-moving air causes the gasoline to evaporate. It turns into a gas and mixes with the air.

The gasoline-air mixture is pulled into the cylinders (SIHL uhn duhrz)—round openings inside the engine. Inside each cylinder is a round part, called a piston (PIHS tuhn), that moves up and down.

As the piston moves up, it squeezes the gasoline-air mixture into the top of the cylinder. Then a hot electric spark shoots into the mixture.

Bang! Instantly, the gas mixture burns. The heat is so fierce and sudden that the molecules rush apart. This is an explosion. The force of the explosion pushes the piston down. The piston pushes on other parts to make them run. The noise you hear when a gasoline engine is running is actually lots of these explosions, one right after another.

This is what happens in the engine of an automobile, a motorcycle, a snowmobile, a lawn mower, and a snow blower. Matter is changed from one form to another—and energy is released to make machines move!

Hot and Cold

You're getting warm

On a chilly day, there's an easy way to make your cold hands feel warmer. Rub them together—fast! Why does rubbing your hands make them warmer?

You are made up of molecules, just like all other kinds of matter around you. The molecules that are *you* hold onto each other very tightly. But they are always moving— jiggling and spinning around. The molecules have energy.

When you rub your hands together, you create friction. You make the molecules in your skin bump and push each other. That bumping and pushing makes the molecules speed up—it gives them more energy. You feel the energy as heat. The faster the molecules move, the warmer you get. So if you rub your hands together hard enough, they won't feel chilly any more. The molecules will move fast enough to make your hands feel warm.

How hot is hot?

Which is hottest—ice cream, a glass of cool water, or a steaming-hot cup of chocolate? Of course, the chocolate is hottest. But it wouldn't be quite right to say that the ice cream and the water aren't hot at all. Each one has some heat.

All things have heat—even very cold things. But some things have more heat than others. So when we use words like *hot* and *cold*, we aren't really talking about two different ideas. We are simply telling how much heat something has.

The molecules in the hot chocolate are moving very fast—they have a lot of energy.

When you swallow those fast-moving molecules, they give you some of their heat energy—they make you feel warm.

And the molecules in the cold ice cream are moving very slowly—but they are moving! They have a small amount of heat energy. Because your body has much *more* heat energy than the ice cream does, ice cream can't warm you up. Instead, it takes away heat energy—it makes you feel cool.

The molecules in cool water move faster than the molecules in ice cream, but they don't move as fast as the molecules in hot chocolate. So, compared to the molecules in ice cream, they are hot—and compared to the molecules in chocolate, they are cold.

Moving molecules

Here is a way to show that hot and cold molecules move at different speeds.

A hot-and-cold contest

Materials

- bowls (2, large)
- food coloring
- medicine dropper
- pan (bigger than bowl)
- water

Fill one bowl with the coldest water you can get from the faucet. Then fill the other bowl with the hottest water you can get. Place both bowls on a table.

Wait until the water stops moving. Then use the medicine dropper to put three drops of food coloring in the center of each bowl. (Don't let the dropper touch the water.) Do this quickly, so that the drops go into each bowl at almost the same time. How fast does the food coloring spread in each bowl?

The food coloring spreads much faster in the hot water than in the cold water. The fast-moving molecules in the hot water spread the molecules of food coloring rapidly.

Warming up

Fill one bowl with very cold water. Place it in the pan. When the water stops moving, put three drops of food coloring in the center of the bowl.

Watch the food coloring spread for fifteen seconds. (You can count slowly to fifteen.) Then pour very hot water into the pan in which the bowl is sitting. What happens?

The food coloring spreads slowly until the hot water is poured into the pan. Then it spreads faster! The hot water outside the bowl heats the cold water in the bowl—it makes the molecules speed up.

How a thermometer works

Is a pool full of ice water warm enough for swimming? Not for you! But for a penguin it might be just right. You and the penguin have different ideas about how "warm" the water is.

You can easily find out how much heat is in

the water. You can measure the temperature of the water with a thermometer (thuhr MAHM uh tuhr).

A thermometer is a closed tube. At one end it has a bulb filled with liquid. When you put the bulb in something—the swimming pool, for instance—the liquid inside the thermometer gets warmer or cooler until it reaches the same temperature as whatever is around it.

If the liquid in the thermometer gets warmer, the molecules speed up and push away from each other. The liquid expands (ehk SPANDZ)—it takes up more space. It pushes out of the bulb and climbs higher in the tube.

If the liquid in the thermometer gets colder, the molecules slow down and move toward each other. The liquid contracts (kuhn TRAKTS)— it takes up less space. It slides down the tube toward the bulb.

The numbers and marks on the thermometer are called degrees (dih GREEZ). They show the amount of heat. When the liquid expands or contracts, the number it reaches is the temperature you are measuring.

So you and the penguin don't have to agree that the water is "cold" or "hot." You can read the thermometer. It will tell you in numbers exactly how hot—or how cold—the water in the pool is.

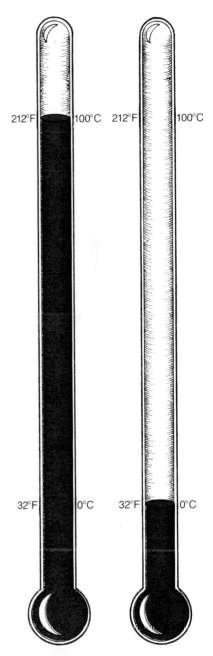

Temperature can be measured in degrees Fahrenheit (F) or degrees Celsius (C). Water boils (left) at 212°F or 100°C. It freezes (right) at 32°F or 0°C.

A solid thermometer

Materials

- cardboard
- foil-and-paper candy wrapper
- pencil
- spool
- tape

Most thermometers you've seen probably use a liquid to measure temperature. But solids can be used to measure heat, too. Solids expand and contract as they get warmer and cooler, just as liquids do. Here's a simple thermometer that measures heat with solids.

Press the candy wrapper as flat as you can. On the paper side, draw a pointer the size of the one shown here. Cut out the pointer.

Tape the straight end of the pointer to the spool. Place the spool on the cardboard, close to one edge. Aim the pointer at the middle of the cardboard. Then tape the spool down. Your thermometer is ready to use.

Take your thermometer to a very cool place and leave it there for a few minutes. Which way does the pointer bend? Make a mark under the pointer and print *C* by it. This is the "cold" end of your temperature scale.

Next leave the thermometer in a very warm spot. Which way does the pointer bend

this time? Make a mark under it and print *H* for the "hot" end of the temperature scale.

Your thermometer works because the metal side of the pointer expands and contracts more than the paper side. In a cold place, it gets shorter than the paper side and pulls the pointer one way. But in a hot place, it gets longer than the paper side and pushes the pointer the other way.

Can you find places with temperatures between *C* and *H?* The direction and distance the pointer bends will show you about how warm or how cool each place is.

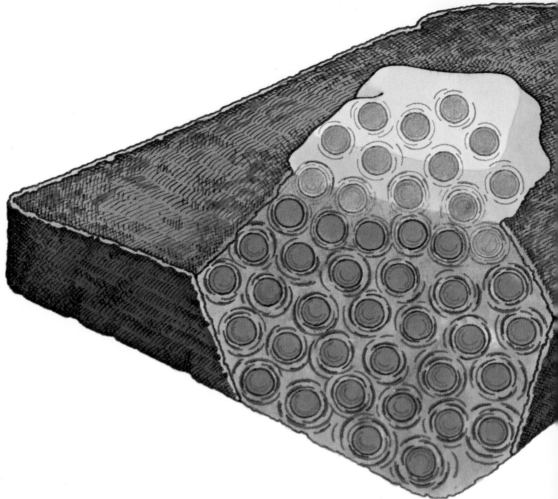

As warm as toast

If you spread cold butter on hot toast, the butter won't stay cold very long. Some of the heat from the toast passes into it. Soon the butter is warm, too—as warm as toast.

Heat energy can spread. It can be conducted (kuhn DUHK tuhd), or carried, from something warmer to something cooler. The movement of molecules passes the heat along.

A slice of toast is a solid piece of bread. But the molecules in the bread move—they jiggle and spin, even though they are held together. As the bread is toasted, the heat

from the toaster makes the molecules speed up. The faster the molecules move, the hotter the toast gets.

Cold butter is a solid, too—its molecules are moving, but they are moving very slowly. When you spread the cold butter on the hot toast, some of the slow-moving butter molecules touch the faster-moving molecules in the toast.

The jiggling toast molecules bump against the slow-moving molecules in the butter. That makes the butter molecules jiggle and spin faster. The fast, jiggling motion spreads from molecule to molecule until all the butter is soft and warm.

When you cook something in a pan, heat is conducted in the same way. The heat from the stove speeds up the molecules of the pan and makes the pan hot. Then the pan conducts heat to the food—its molecules bump against the food molecules and speed them up until the food gets hot, too.

Little blocks of water

Why does lemonade get cooler when you put ice cubes in it? The answer may surprise you. The lemonade cools down because it heats up the ice!

Ice cubes are a solid—little blocks of frozen water. The water molecules in ice cubes have very little heat energy. They move very slowly, and they pull very hard on each other.

There are water molecules in the lemonade, too. But even in very cold lemonade, the water molecules move much faster than molecules of solid ice. They have much more heat energy than the ice does.

When you put ice cubes in lemonade, the fast-moving molecules in the lemonade bump against the slow-moving molecules in the ice. Bit by bit, they make the molecules on the outside of the ice cubes speed up. When the molecules are moving fast enough, the ice begins to melt—it changes from a solid to a liquid and mixes with the lemonade in the glass.

But ice molecules need a lot of energy to melt. They get that heat energy from the lemonade. As the molecules in the lemonade lose their heat energy, they slow down. They bump against each other less and less, and the lemonade gets cool.

As long as there is ice in the glass, heat energy moves from the lemonade to the ice

cubes. So your lemonade stays cold until all
the ice is melted. When there is no more ice
to take up heat energy, all of the lemonade in
the glass gets warm.

What makes a teakettle whistle?

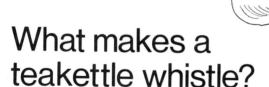

You don't have to watch a whistling teakettle to know when the water is hot. The kettle will "tell" you when the water begins to boil. The kettle makes a long, loud whistle.

When *you* whistle, you push air out through a small opening that you make with your lips. The whistling sound of the kettle is made in almost the same way. But the push that makes the kettle whistle doesn't come from air. It comes from steam.

As the water inside the kettle is heated, the molecules take up energy. That energy makes the molecules speed up and push hard against each other. When the water is hot enough, some of it changes from a liquid to a gas. It turns to steam.

Because the molecules are pushing hard against each other, the steam expands—it takes up much more space than the hot water did. It pushes against the inside of the kettle. But there is only one place where it can escape—through the small hole in the spout. So it squeezes out with a hard push, and the push makes a whistle.

When a large amount of water is boiled, the push from expanding steam can be very strong. If the steam isn't allowed to escape, it can be used to push the moving parts of machines—to run ships, trains, and power plants that make electricity.

Tricks with heat

These tricks aren't really magic—they just *look* mysterious. Heat energy makes them work.

Water ballet

You can entertain your friends with a water show small enough to fit into a mixing bowl. The real performers are the ice cubes!

Materials

- crayons
- ice-cube tray
- mixing bowl (large)
- paper
- scissors
- water

Draw and cut out some tiny performers the size of the ones shown here. Use your crayons to color both sides.

Fill the ice-cube tray half full with water. Put the tray in the freezer until a little ice forms on top. Then take the tray out and lay a "performer" on each cube.

Carefully pour in more water until the tray is full. Then freeze the cubes until they are solid.

To put on a water show, fill a large bowl

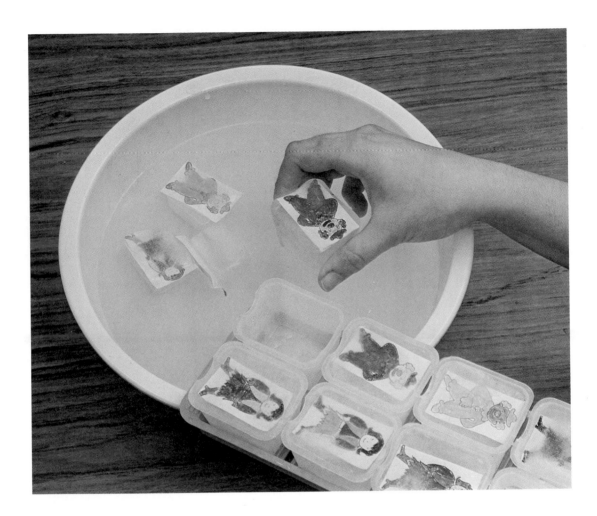

with warm water. Then put two or three cubes in the bowl. In a minute or two the tiny ice-cube figures will begin to flip and turn.

What makes the figures turn over? When you put the ice cubes in warm water, the bottom of each cube begins to melt. The molecules mix with the water in the bowl. Soon the top of the ice cube is bigger and heavier than the bottom. So the ice cube flips over. As the new bottom side melts, the ice cube flips again.

Which coin?

Materials

- box
- pennies (5, with different dates)

Have some friends help you with this trick. They'll give you the answer without knowing that they have!

Show your friends five pennies in a small box. Explain that you can read your friends' minds—that you can tell which coin they choose.

While your back is turned, have your friends choose one of the coins and remember the date. Then ask each friend to hold the coin tightly in one hand for a moment and concentrate hard on the date. When everyone has had a turn, have the last person drop the coin in the box.

As soon as the coin is returned to the box,

turn around and touch each coin lightly. Four of the coins will be cool—but the fifth will be warm, because it has taken heat energy from your friends' hands. Pretend to think very hard for a moment—and then surprise everyone by picking out the right coin.

Color up

Does water ever flow up? Yes, it does—and you can prove it to your friends.

Put three drops of food coloring in one bottle. Fill the bottle with the hottest water you can get from the faucet. Then fill the other bottle with cold water.

Place the card over the top of the bottle of cold water. Holding the card firmly, turn the bottle upside down. Making sure the water doesn't spill, place the bottle on top of the bottle of hot water. Line the bottles up exactly. Then pull out the card.

In a moment a stream of the hot colored water will climb into the bottle of cold water. Hot water is lighter than cold water. The molecules in hot water move faster and are farther apart than the molecules in cold water. So, when the bottles are joined, the hot water pushes upward. It rises into the heavier, colder water above it.

Materials

- bottles (2, large)
- card (thin)
- food coloring
- water

Going up!

Do you know that some people use a bag of hot air to fly? They really do. The "bag" is a huge hot-air balloon. The balloon can lift people because hot air behaves in a special way.

When air is heated, its molecules speed up and begin to push on each other, just like the molecules of solids and liquids. This makes the air expand.

Because air is a gas, its molecules move much more freely than the molecules of a solid or a liquid. So heated air expands much more than does a heated solid or liquid. The molecules of hot air push farther and farther apart until only a few molecules take up a great deal of space.

The hot air that fills a balloon has many fewer molecules than the colder air outside the balloon. So, the hot air actually weighs much less than the colder air. Because the hot air is lighter, it rises. It pushes up inside the balloon—and when the push is strong enough, it lifts the balloon and keeps it floating in the heavier, colder air outside.

Heating the air in your house won't make the house float away. But it does make the air rise. The warmer, lighter air from a stove or furnace flows upward toward the ceiling, spreading heat through the rooms. Then, as the air loses heat energy, it cools down. As it sinks toward the floor, other warm air takes its place.

Weighing air

You can make a scale with which to weigh air! A lamp with an ordinary light bulb will make the warm air you need.

Balance one stick between two chairs or two small tables. Make sure the stick is steady.

Cut two pieces of string. Tape one end of each piece of string to the bottom of a paper bag. Then tie one bag to each end of the second stick. Open the bags all the way.

Balance the second stick across the first stick. Make sure that the stick is straight and that the bags hang down evenly.

Turn on the lamp. Stand it under one of the paper bags, so that the heat from the light bulb warms the air in the bag. What happens as the air gets warm?

When the air inside one bag warms up, the two bags are no longer balanced. The bag above the lamp moves up, and the other bag moves down.

The heated air in the bag above the lamp expands as it warms up—the molecules push farther and farther away from each other. Some of the air is pushed out of the bag.

The air left in the warm-air bag has many fewer molecules than the air in the cool-air bag. It weighs much less than the cool air. So the bag of warm, light air rises, and the bag of heavy, cool air sinks.

Materials

- lamp
- paper bags (2, same size)
- sticks (2, long)
- string
- tape

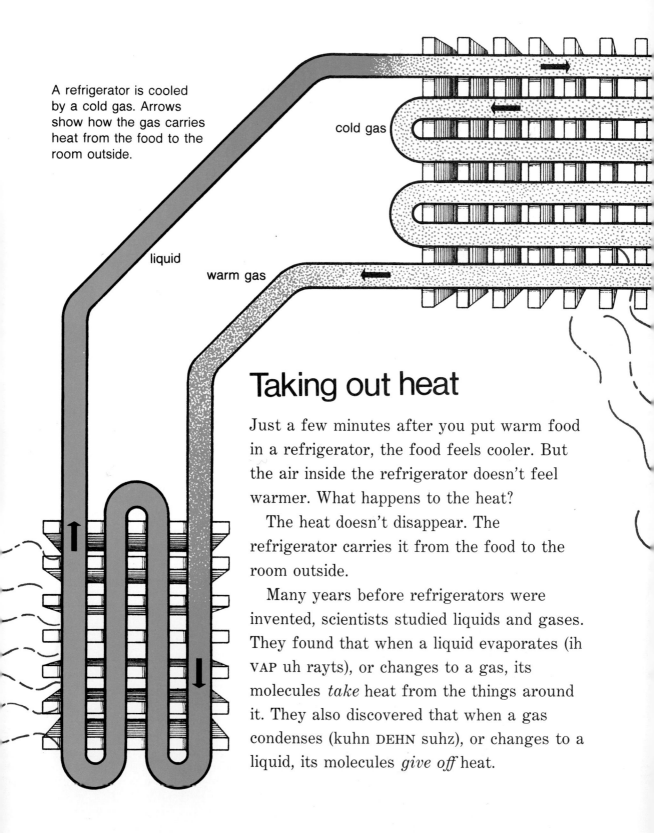

A refrigerator is cooled by a cold gas. Arrows show how the gas carries heat from the food to the room outside.

cold gas

liquid

warm gas

Taking out heat

Just a few minutes after you put warm food in a refrigerator, the food feels cooler. But the air inside the refrigerator doesn't feel warmer. What happens to the heat?

The heat doesn't disappear. The refrigerator carries it from the food to the room outside.

Many years before refrigerators were invented, scientists studied liquids and gases. They found that when a liquid evaporates (ih VAP uh rayts), or changes to a gas, its molecules *take* heat from the things around it. They also discovered that when a gas condenses (kuhn DEHN suhz), or changes to a liquid, its molecules *give off* heat.

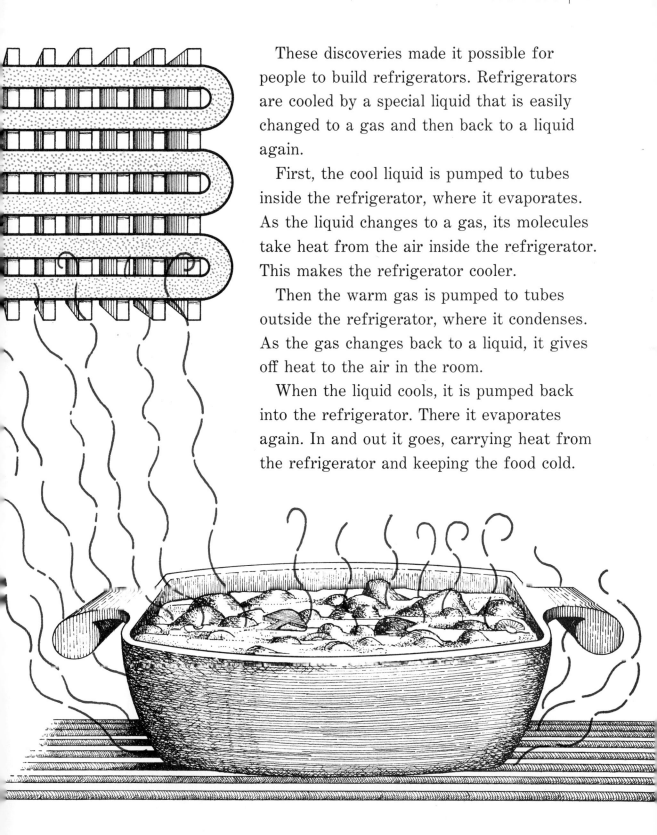

These discoveries made it possible for people to build refrigerators. Refrigerators are cooled by a special liquid that is easily changed to a gas and then back to a liquid again.

First, the cool liquid is pumped to tubes inside the refrigerator, where it evaporates. As the liquid changes to a gas, its molecules take heat from the air inside the refrigerator. This makes the refrigerator cooler.

Then the warm gas is pumped to tubes outside the refrigerator, where it condenses. As the gas changes back to a liquid, it gives off heat to the air in the room.

When the liquid cools, it is pumped back into the refrigerator. There it evaporates again. In and out it goes, carrying heat from the refrigerator and keeping the food cold.

The Fire Bringer

A Paiute Indian legend
Adapted from a story by Mary Austin

The use of fire is probably the most important discovery people ever made. It provided energy for light, for warmth, and for cooking. People used fire to make their lives easier and more comfortable.

Tales of how fire was first discovered have grown up in every land. People everywhere thought of fire as a gift from the gods. This Paiute Indian legend shows how highly the gift of fire was valued.

There was a time, long, long ago, when the Paiute people did not have fire.

In summer, this did not matter, for the land of the Paiutes was warm. The people didn't wear much clothing. They did not even need houses. They moved about the land, gathering food. The women and girls used sharp sticks to dig up tasty roots. With nets made of twisted tree bark, men and boys caught bright fish in the streams. There was laughter and happiness. All was well.

But in winter, things were very different. The air was bitter cold and heavy snow lay upon the land. The people wrapped themselves in robes made of woven rabbit skins and huddled together in their underground pit-houses. They were miserable and unhappy.

Among the Paiute there was one boy who was as cold as anyone. But he thought only of the others. It bothered him to see his people so unhappy.

One day, as the boy sat huddled on a snowy hillside, Coyote came to him. In those days, men and animals could talk to one another, and Coyote was the Friend and Counselor of man.

"Why are you troubled, boy?" Coyote asked.

"I sorrow for my people," answered the boy. "They are suffering from the cold."

"I do not feel it," said Coyote.

"That is because you have a coat of fur," the boy said. "The only fur my people have, they must get by hunting. And this is not easy. Is there no way to help them?"

"There is a way—there is something that can be done," said Coyote. "It will be very hard to do, but I will help you. We must bring fire to your people."

The boy stared at him. "Fire? What is fire?"

Coyote thought for a time, wondering how best to describe fire to someone who had never seen it. "It is like a bright, red flower, yet it is not a flower," he said. "Nor is it a beast, even though, like a beast, it runs through grass and woods and devours everything in its path. It is fierce, and can cause pain. But if it is kept inside a circle of stones, and fed with small sticks, it will be a friend to your people. It will give them light, keep them warm, and cook their food."

"Where is this fire?" asked the boy. "How can we get it?"

"Its den is on the Burning Mountain by the Big Water, more than a hundred days journey from here," Coyote told him. "It is guarded day and night by the Fire Spirits. No man can get near it. But the Fire Spirits will not pay any attention to an animal, for animals are known to fear fire. Perhaps I can creep close enough to steal some of the fire and give it to you."

The boy leaped to his feet. "Let us go, my friend," he cried.

"Wait," warned Coyote. "I told you that it will not be easy. The Fire Spirits will chase us, and they are swift as the rushing wind. You could never run for a hundred days without them catching you! You must have help. There must be a hundred of your tribe's swiftest runners, each waiting a day's distance apart."

"I will get them," declared the boy.

He went among his people and told them of the things Coyote had said. He urged them to help him get fire. But some were afraid, others were lazy, and many simply did not believe him. "How can you, who are only a boy, know about this 'fire'?" they asked, scornfully. "We have never heard of it."

But the boy pleaded and argued. Finally, the people decided that they were so cold and unhappy they had nothing to lose. They might as well do as the boy wanted. They chose the tribe's hundred swiftest runners. Then, led by the boy and Coyote, the people started out.

They left the place of their home and went into the great mountains whose peaks reached up out of the snow and touched the sky. They followed the mountain streams down through a long stretch of dark, frightening forest. They came to a vast, parched plain, where the dried earth had broken into countless cracks, and the horizon was hidden in a blue mist.

At the end of each day, Coyote told one of the runners to stay behind. "Wait here," he said. "In time, you will see a man running toward you, carrying a stick upon which a bright, red flower is growing. But it will not be a flower, it will be fire. You must take the stick from him and run as fast as you can to where the next runner is waiting."

One by one, the runners were left behind. Finally at the end of the hundredth day, Coyote and the boy stood at the foot of the Burning Mountain. It was a great, black cone, and from its point rose a plume of smoke. As the sky darkened with night, the top of the mountain glowed. And the glare of the fire turned the waves of the Big Water red when the Fire Spirits began their dance.

"I will go now and try to steal a bit of fire,"
said Coyote. "When you see me coming back,
be ready to run. The Fire Spirits will be chasing
me, and I will be too tired to go on. You must
take the fire from me and carry it to the next
runner."

Then Coyote picked up a dry branch and
started up the mountainside. His fur was dirty
and he was thin from the long way he had come.
The Fire Spirits laughed to see this shabby,
skinny, slinking creature, so hungry he was

chewing on an old tree branch. They paid no more attention to him—which was exactly what Coyote wanted.

As the Fire Spirits began to dance, Coyote crouched and waited. Then he leaped forward and caught a bit of fire on the branch. Holding the burning branch in his mouth, he dashed away. He raced down the mountainside as fast as his legs could carry him. Hissing and crackling with rage, the Fire Spirits rushed after him.

The boy saw Coyote coming, and saw the red flower glowing on the branch in Coyote's mouth. He also saw the burning sparks streaming back along Coyote's sides, and he heard the singing sound of the enraged Fire Spirits close behind. He braced himself, like an arrow in a bent bow, ready to fly.

Coyote reached him nearly out of breath. The boy took the burning branch and began to run. Through the night and into the next day he ran, the Fire Spirits snapping and singing behind him. Gasping for breath and about to drop, he finally reached the next runner and handed him the flaming branch.

And so the torch was passed from one man to another. Runners sped over the parched plain and through the dark woods. Behind them hissed the furious Fire Spirits. But when they reached the snowy mountains, the Fire Spirits stopped. They could not go on, for fire cannot live on snow.

Finally, the last runner brought the burning branch back to his own land. The people surrounded the fire with a circle of stones. And they fed it twigs, as Coyote had told them to.

The fire blazed up and burned cheerfully. The people crowded about, marveling at the light and warmth and comfort it gave them. In time, they learned to use it to cook their food as well, which made the food taste better.

As for the boy, the people named him the Fire Bringer. He was called by this name until

he died. Then, the Paiute people named Coyote
the Fire Bringer, because there was no one else
with so good a right to the name.

The Paiute people know this tale is true. Look
at any thin, shabby, slinking coyote. You can
see for yourself that the fur on its sides looks
as if it were singed by the fire brought down
from the Burning Mountain.

How does a
picnic cooler work?

What kinds of food can you take on a picnic?
Any kinds you like—hot baked beans,
steaming cocoa, chilled potato salad, or ice-
cold lemonade. You can put the food in a
picnic cooler, or in special dishes or bottles, to
keep it cold or warm.

Foods packed in these special containers
are insulated (IHN suh layt uhd). They are
surrounded by layers of matter that keep
heat in or out.

Some kinds of matter, such as aluminum, steel, and other metals, conduct heat very well. Their molecules move very easily and pass the heat along.

But other kinds of matter have molecules that move very little. They conduct heat very slowly—so slowly that sometimes they hardly seem to carry heat at all.

Materials like wood, cork, and plastic foam don't conduct heat very well. So containers made with these materials are used to slow down heat! When you pack hot food in an insulated dish, it loses heat very slowly. And when you pack cold food in a picnic cooler, the heat from the outside air takes a long time to get in.

The same kinds of materials are used to insulate houses and other buildings. In cold weather, the insulation slows down the heat going *out* and helps keep buildings warm. And in hot weather, insulation slows down the heat coming *in* and helps the houses and buildings stay cool.

Heat-savers

What kinds of materials can be used to slow down heat? You can use your refrigerator to make an easy test.

Make sure there is enough room in the bottom of the freezing compartment in your refrigerator to hold the materials you test.

Cut a small square from the aluminum foil and the paper, and a piece about the same size from the plastic foam cup. Now you are ready to make the test.

Place these pieces, as well as the marble, penny, quarter, and wooden button, in the freezing compartment. Make sure that they do not touch each other. Close the refrigerator door and wait five minutes.

Open the refrigerator and lightly touch each thing with a *different* finger. Which ones feel coldest?

The aluminum foil, the penny, and the quarter will feel coldest. Because they are metal, they are good conductors of heat. So they lose heat quickly in the cold freezing compartment.

The glass marble will not feel as cold as the metal things. And the paper, the wooden button, and the plastic foam will hardly feel cold at all. Glass, wood, paper, and plastic foam are poor conductors, so they are good insulators. They can be used to slow down the movement of heat.

Seeing
the Light

What is light?

A burning candle has a soft, glowing flame that gives off light. But when you turn on a light bulb, there is no flame. What makes the light bulb give off light?

If you hold your hand above a light bulb, you'll find a clue. The bulb is hot! When the light is on, electricity runs through a tiny wire inside the bulb. This makes the wire get hot. And when the wire gets hot enough, something begins to happen.

Like everything else, the wire is made of atoms. And in the atoms there are electrons. As the wires in the light bulb get hot, the electrons soak up energy. And when they are loaded with energy, they throw it off. The

bundles of energy thrown off by the electrons are light.

The bundles of energy have a special name. They are called *photons* (FOH tahnz). *Photo* is a word part that means "light," and *on* at the end means "a bit." So photons are "bits of light."

Anything that is hot enough—the tiny wire in the light bulb, a candle flame, or a log fire—gives off light. And something as big and as hot as the sun gives off a tremendous amount of light. The sun has a temperature millions of times hotter than a light bulb, a candle flame, or anything on earth. So the sun keeps its electrons jumping. And the electrons keep pouring out bundles and bundles of light.

Looking at moonlight

Boys and girls, come out to play,
The moon is shining bright as day.
Mother Goose

Under a full moon there is plenty of light for a game of tag, for hide-and-seek, or for an evening walk. It's almost as easy to see on a bright moonlit night as it is by day.

But the moon doesn't really give off the bright, silvery light that we see. The moon shines only because the sun shines on it. Some of the sun's light bounces off the moon and is reflected to the earth. So we think of it as moonlight—even though what we see is really light from the sun.

Some of the things we see—light bulbs, neon signs, traffic lights, and even TV tubes—are like the sun. They give off light. But most of the things we see are like the moon. They don't give off light of their own. Light from the sun, a lamp, or some other place shines on them. Then we see them. They reflect the light into our eyes, and the reflected light tells us what shapes, sizes, and colors the things are.

Light gets around

Materials

- ball (small)
- block (small)
- cardboard
- clay (modeling)
- flashlight
- jar (round)
- masking tape
- milk
- mirror (small)
- paper (white)
- ruler
- scissors
- water

The instant you turn on a lamp, the room is bright. Light seems to be everywhere at once. Light moves faster than anything we know of. It can travel from the moon to the earth in less than a second!

Light moves in a straight line. But some things will make it bend. Some things will block it. And some things will make it bounce back. Here's a project that will show you how light travels and how some things affect it.

First, measure and cut eight strips of cardboard. These should be five inches (20 centimeters) long and three-quarters of an inch (2 cm) wide.

Next, lay the strips out side by side, leaving a one-eighth inch (0.3 cm) space between the strips. Use the ruler to help you make the spaces even.

Put something heavy across the strips to keep them in place, or have a friend hold them down so they won't slide apart. Tape the strips together at the top and bottom. Then turn them over and tape the other side. Trim off any extra tape from the ends. Bend the end strips back so that the card will stand up.

With the card, and the other things you have collected, you are ready to find out more about how light behaves. Take your things to a dark room.

Keeping it straight

Put the sheet of white paper on a table, or on the floor, and stand the card on it. Hold the flashlight about four inches from the card and shine it at the middle slit. Where does the light go?

Light shines through each slit in a straight beam. None of the beams bend or touch each other. But each beam of light spreads a little as it travels.

Getting together

Now fill the jar with water and place it on the other side of the card. Shine the light through the slits into the jar. What happens to the light now?

This time the light doesn't spread! It comes together at one point on the other side of the jar.

To see what is happening, add a few drops of milk—just enough to make the water cloudy. Can you see the light beams? Where do they go?

The light beams bend toward each other when they enter the water. Then, as they leave the water, they bend even more. They come together, or focus, just outside the jar.

Nowhere to go

Place the block in back of the card, so that it touches the card. Shine the light through the slits again. Which slits let the light through? Where is the light stopped?

Do the same thing using the ball instead of the block. What happens?

The light is stopped wherever part of the block or the ball is in back of the slits. Where nothing is in back of the slits, the light goes through. The ball and the block are different shapes, so they stop the beams of light in different places.

Bounce, bounce

Stand a small mirror on the other side of the card, about four inches (10 cm) from it. Use a lump of clay to hold it in place. Make sure the mirror is straight. Now shine the light through the slits. What happens? Turn the mirror a little to one side. What happens to the light beams this time?

When the light beams hit the mirror, they bounce back. If they hit the mirror straight, they bounce back straight. But if they hit the mirror at a slant, they bounce away from it at a slant.

What makes a shadow?

In the sunshine, your shadow travels with you everywhere you go. Sometimes it bends in funny places. Sometimes it takes a strange shape. But it's always there. On a cloudy day, or in a dark room, you have no shadow at all. What is your shadow? Where does your shadow go?

We have shadows because light moves in a certain way. It travels outward from its source. It moves in waves, something like ripples in water. As long as nothing is in the way, the light waves move in one direction. But when some of the light waves hit something—you, or a tree, or a house—they are stopped. Then, on the other side of the thing that stopped the light waves, there is a dark space—a shadow.

Things in a dark room have no shadows because there are no light waves traveling through the room. And on cloudy days, things have no shadows because the clouds break up the light waves from the sun. The clouds soak up some of the waves and scatter the rest of them in all directions. When the light waves scatter and bounce instead of moving in one direction, no shadows are formed.

Shadow time

Materials

- clock
- glue
- paper plate
- pencil (long)
- pencil (for marking)
- ruler
- spool

At sunrise your shadow on the ground is very long—longer than you are! At sunset your shadow is long again, but it points the other way. And in the middle of the day, when the sun is high in the sky, your shadow is very short—it's just a small, dark spot around your feet.

The way shadows change can help you tell the time. You can make a shadow clock.

Glue the spool to the middle of the paper plate. Then stand the pencil in the hole in the spool, with the point up. Draw a small arrow on the edge of the plate.

Find a window, or a spot outdoors, where there is sunlight for a long time—all day, if possible. Put the paper plate there. Make sure the arrow points south.

Look at the time early in the morning. When the clock reaches the nearest hour, use the ruler to draw a line down the shadow the pencil makes on the paper plate. Write the hour next to the line you traced.

Do the same thing every hour. Check the timo, draw a linc down the shadow, and wriile the hour next to the line. The last line you can draw on your clock is thc last hour before the sun goes down.

When you have a line for each hour of sunlight, your shadow clock is finished. You can use it to tell time on any sunny day. Put it in the sun, making sure that the arrow points south. The shadow of the pencil will point to the time of day.

Mirror, mirror

Who is that person in the mirror? It seems to be another you, doing exactly what you are doing. How can a mirror "copy" you?

A mirror is very smooth. The front of a mirror is flat, polished glass. Behind the glass is a thin layer of silver or some other kind of shiny material.

As you stand in front of a mirror, light bounces off you and passes through the glass.

When the light hits the shiny layer behind the glass, it bounces straight back. This is why you can see yourself.

Your reflection is a good copy of you. But have you ever tried to shake hands with it? You can't. When you hold out your right hand, your reflection holds out its left hand. You can't march in step with it, either. When you step with your left foot, your reflection steps with its right foot.

Why does your reflection do just the opposite of what you do? Pretend for a moment that the mirror is something you could fall into—like a soft blanket of fresh snow. If you fall into the snowbank face down, you leave a perfect "print" of yourself. Your "snow print" is like your reflection in the mirror. Your right hand makes the left hand of your "snow print," and your left hand makes the print's right hand. Your right foot makes the print's left foot, and your left foot makes the print's right foot.

A mirror works in the same way. The light bounces straight off each part of you and into the mirror. The shiny surface behind the glass bounces the light straight back. So the reflection you see is a "light print." Each part of you makes the opposite part of your reflection in the mirror.

What do you think will happen if you print your name and hold it up to a mirror? Try it and see.

Close-ups

Its huge, glittering eyes stare at you. Its big
mouth opens and closes, opens and closes.
But suddenly it swims to the other side of the
bowl. It's only a small goldfish, after all!

Why did the goldfish look so big when it
swam next to the curved glass? The bowl
filled with water acted as a lens. It *bent* the
light that bounced off the goldfish and came
through the bowl. This made the goldfish look
much bigger than it really is.

Most of the lenses we use are made of plastic or glass. But anything can be a lens if it is curved and if light can pass through it. A curved shape makes light bend and spread. And spreading the light that bounces off a thing makes that thing look bigger. A lens with the right curve will make something look larger or closer than it really is.

A magnifying glass is just a single lens with two curved sides. You can use it for a close-up look at things like paper or cloth or even your finger. Move it up and down until

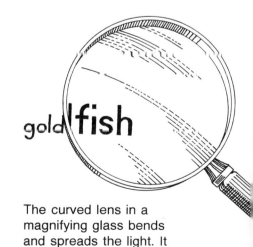

gold**fish**

The curved lens in a magnifying glass bends and spreads the light. It makes things look bigger than they really are.

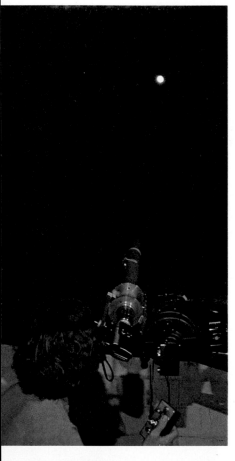

it is the right distance from what you are looking at. You will get a sharp, clear view—and what you see may surprise you.

A microscope gives you close-ups of very small things. It lets you see things that are so tiny you couldn't see them with your eyes alone. A microscope has two sets of lenses. These are lined up in a tube that can be moved up and down. When the lenses are the right distance from the thing you are looking at, they spread the light just as the magnifying glass does. But with two sets of lenses, whatever you look at is magnified twice. It looks much larger than it really is.

A telescope makes faraway things seem close. The simplest kind of telescope has two lenses in a tube, something like a microscope. Part of the telescope moves in and out to change the distance between the lenses. When the distance is right, a clear picture is formed.

In big telescopes, light from the sky shines down a tube onto a large, curved mirror. The mirror takes the place of the first lens—it gathers and bends the light. It reflects the picture up to a smaller mirror. This smaller mirror reflects the picture through a lens to your eye. With one of these telescopes, you can see faraway planets and stars.

A telescope gives you a close-up view of faraway things, like the moon.

A water-drop lens

You can make a lens from anything that is curved and clear—even a drop of water. Here is an easy way to make a magnifying lens.

Cut a hole about the size of a large coin in the cardboard. Cover the hole with a piece of food wrap. Stretch the wrap as smooth as you can and tape it down.

Find a newspaper page with a picture. Lay the cardboard on the picture. Use the dropper to put one drop of water on the wrap. Look at the picture through the water drop. What you see may surprise you.

The picture is made up of tiny dots. In the darkest parts, the dots are very close together. Where the picture is lighter, the dots are farther apart. For a better view, raise the lens. The dots will look larger.

You'll find that the printing and the paper look different, too. The "smooth" paper is fuzzy, and the edges of letters are rough.

Materials

- cardboard
- food wrap (clear plastic)
- medicine dropper
- scissors
- tape
- water

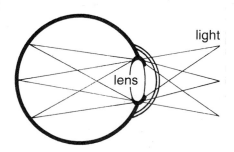

The lens in your eye bends light rays and makes them focus, or come together, at the back of your eye.

Seeing it clearly

Your eyes don't hurt, but the doctor says you need glasses. Why? How can glasses help your eyes?

Light comes into your eye through the pupil—the round, dark opening in the middle. Just behind the pupil is a built-in lens. The lens bends the light and makes it fall on a spot called the retina (REHT uh nuh) that is at the back of the eye. The retina is full of nerves that go to your brain. When light touches the retina, a message is sent to your brain—and you see.

The lenses in your eyes are soft. They change shape, so that light rays will come together, or focus, on the retina. Muscles in the eye squeeze the lens and make it thicker for close-up seeing. For far-off seeing, muscles pull the lens and make it thinner.

Sometimes people's eyes are not quite the right shape. No squeezing or pulling changes the lens enough to make the light rays focus on the retina. Either nearby or faraway things look fuzzy.

When your eyes are tested, the doctor can tell exactly how much help your lenses need. Then glasses are made with lenses that bend the light rays just enough to make them focus on the retina.

Glowing eyes

Silently the tiger crouches, its striped coat blending perfectly with the evening shadows. A deer is coming! The tiger turns its head to watch—and suddenly its eyes begin to glow with a strange light.

The tiger can't really make its eyes glow. Its eyes are very much like yours. They have a curving, transparent window called the *cornea* (KAWR nee uh) just in front of the dark spot at the middle, and a built-in lens just behind the dark spot. The cornea and the lens gather light and bend it, so that it reaches the back of the eye.

But tigers, cats, dogs, and some other hunting animals need to see clearly at night as well as by day. Their eyes have a mirrorlike layer at the back. At night the layer catches the very dim light that comes in and reflects it forward inside the eye. The reflected light helps the animals to see.

Sometimes in a dim light a cat will turn its head and look at you from just the right angle. Then you see the strange glow—the light reflecting from the special layer in the cat's eyes.

Smile for the camera

There you are with that stuffed bear you had when you were two. And here you are with that big fish you caught last summer. Both times someone took your picture. The camera made a copy of the way you looked.

A camera "sees" pictures almost the way you do. It has a lens that acts like the lens in your eye. The lens gathers the light and bends it, so that it falls on the film inside. The light "prints" a picture on the film.

The shutter acts like your eyelid—but most of the time the shutter is closed. When you press a button, the shutter winks open for just a small part of a second to let the light hit the film.

Before you take a picture, you push a lever or wind a knob. The last picture you took moves out of the way and a new part of the film moves into place. Next you look through a window called a viewfinder to see what will be in the picture. Finally you press the button. Wink—the shutter opens and closes. When the film is developed, you'll have a picture you can keep   a picture that shows what you and the camera saw.

The lens of a camera bends light rays so that they focus, or come together, on the film. It is the light rays that "print" the picture on the film.

Dark-room pictures

Materials

- blanket or cloth (heavy)
- coffee can
- hammer
- nail (small)
- rubber band
- waxed paper

What does the camera "see" when you take a picture? You can't climb inside it to find out. But you can make a viewer called a camera obscura that will show you a picture as a camera would view it.

Camera is Latin for "room," and *obscura* (ahb SKYOOR uh) is Latin for "dark." That's exactly what the first camera obscura was—a dark room made for viewing. But your camera obscura will be much smaller than a room.

First, turn the coffee can upside down. Use the hammer and the nail to punch a small hole in the center of the bottom. The smaller and smoother the hole is, the sharper the picture will be. So try not to let the nail wiggle or bend when you pound it.

Now turn the can right side up. Cut a piece of waxed paper big enough to cover the top. Put the waxed paper over the top of the can and fasten it in place with the rubber band. Try to keep the paper as smooth and tight as possible.

Find a window with a bright, sunny view. Set your camera obscura so that the hole faces the window. Now put the blanket over your head and the part of the coffee can nearest you. Keep your eyes about a foot from the waxed paper. Move the can until it points at something that is in bright sunlight. You will see a picture of that thing on the waxed paper—but the picture will be small, and it will be upside down.

And that is what your camera "sees"! Light waves coming in through the lens cross each other. A small, upside-down picture reaches the film when you snap the shutter. After the film is developed, a print of the picture is made. And, of course, the picture you get is right side up.

196

Colors we see

The cheese in your sandwich is orange. The tomato is bright red. The lettuce is green. The light brown bread has a dark brown crust. You would be surprised if your sandwich had red cheese, a brown tomato,

Light shining through a prism makes a rainbow.

orange lettuce, and light green bread with a dark green crust. In fact, you might not feel very hungry!

We see colors in things because of the way things reflect light. White light is a mixture of all colors. You can see these colors if you shine bright sunlight through a special glass called a prism.

When white light goes through a prism, it spreads and separates into a rainbowlike band of colors. If you look carefully, you should be able to see six bands of color, each one blending into the next. The colors are violet, blue, green, yellow, orange, and, finally, red.

When white light shines on something, some of the colors are absorbed, or soaked up. Other colors are reflected. The tomato in your sandwich looks red because it absorbs other colors and reflects red. Lettuce absorbs other colors and reflects green. The cheese reflects orange light. And the bread reflects a mixture of colors that your eyes see as brown.

The paper on this page looks white because it reflects all of the colors in white light. Nearly all the light bounces off the paper and reaches your eyes. The words look black because they reflect almost no light at all. Black things absorb nearly all the light that reaches them. So you don't see any color in something that is black.

A rainbow of colors

Sunsets and traffic lights, campfires and TV screens—light comes in many different colors. What makes the colors different? Why do we see a rainbow of colors?

All the colors of light are given off in the same way. When atoms are heated, the electrons soak up energy. Then they give off the energy as photons—bundles of light.

But electrons don't always give off the same amount of energy. An electron behaves somewhat like a ball that you toss from hand to hand. If you toss the ball gently, it falls softly—*pat*—into your hand. But if you put all your energy into a hard throw—*whap!* The ball hits hard and makes your hand sting.

Sometimes electrons take up only a little energy. The photons they give off then are small bundles of energy, like the "pat" the ball makes in your hand. But if electrons take up a lot of energy, the photons they give off have more energy. They are like the "whap" of a hard-thrown ball.

Photons in red light are like "pats." The energy bundles are smaller than in any other color. Photons in violet light are like "whaps." They have more energy than any other color. And the photons of all the other colors are in between. Each kind of photon has its own "pat" or "whap"—a certain amount of energy.

Colors we don't see

Ouch! When you went swimming, the sun wasn't very bright and the air wasn't very hot. But now you have a stinging sunburn! Where did you get it?

Your sunburn came from light—but not from light that you can see.

When all the colors in sunlight are separated, they make a rainbow. The rainbow has a band of red on one edge and a band of violet on the other edge. In between are all the other colors. But beyond the red edge and the violet edge of the rainbow, there are "colors" you don't see!

A suntan comes from ultraviolet (uhl truh VY uh liht) rays—and a sunburn does, too. *Ultraviolet* means "beyond violet." Ultraviolet rays are just beyond the violet edge of the rainbow. You can't see these rays. But you can see what they do. Their energy can make your skin darker or give you a sunburn, even on a cloudy day.

The heat you feel when the sun is bright comes from infrared (in fruh REHD) rays. *Infrared* means "below red." Infrared rays are just below the red edge of the rainbow. These rays can't be seen, either. But you can feel them. When they hit something, the energy they give off makes the thing heat up. Sidewalks get hot in summer because they absorb energy from the sun's infrared rays.

When you sit under a sun lamp, you get a tan from ultraviolet rays. The sun lamp gives off light that you can see. But it also has an extra part that gives off invisible rays of ultraviolet light.

And when you stand near a heat lamp on a chilly evening, you also soak up invisible rays. Infrared rays from the lamp give off energy when they reach you. You feel the energy of the infrared rays as the heat that keeps you warm.

Seeing things
that aren't there

Can a lake vanish? A few minutes ago you
saw cool water shimmering just up the road
ahead of the car. But now all you see is miles
of hot paved highway. Where is the lake?

The disappearing lake is a mirage (muh
RAHZH)—something that isn't where it seems
to be. The mirage is made by light reflected
from something far away. You can see a
mirage only when there are layers of cool air
and warm air close to the earth.

Light usually travels in a straight line. But
when light passes through layers of warm
and cool air, it behaves differently. The warm
and cool layers act like a lens. They bend the
light.

If the bottom layer of air is warm, the
mirage will be close to the earth. But if the
bottom layer is cold, the light will bend the
other way. The mirage will be high up—it
may even seem to float in the air!

A mirage can come from surprising places.
A "lake" may be light waves from far-off
clouds. A rocky "island" may be light waves
from a distant mountaintop. People at sea
have even spotted "ghost ships" floating
upside down in the sky—mirages of real ships
far away on another part of the ocean. And
in the Strait of Messina, off the coast of

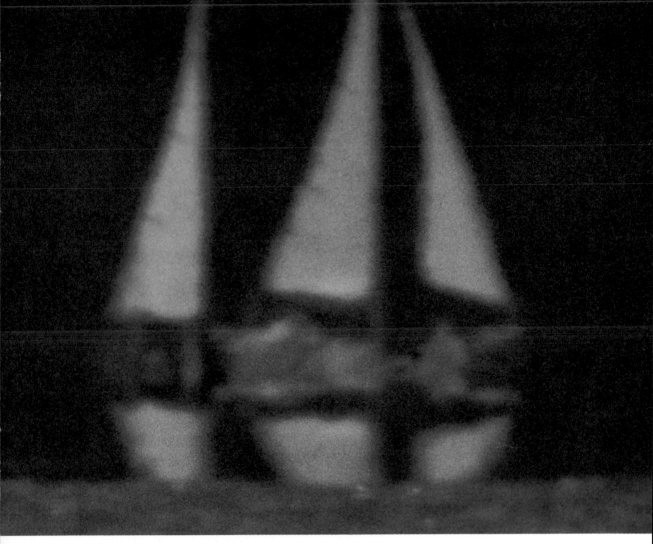

The water in this picture is real, but the sailboat and its reflection are both mirages.

Sicily, an "enchanted city" sometimes appears. It seems to be floating in the water!

You can never reach a mirage, because what you see isn't really there. But the light waves you see *are* real. If you have a camera, you can take a picture of the mirage. The camera will "see" the light waves just as you do—and you will have a picture of the thing that isn't there!

Eyes for machines

Sometimes only a few people get on and off the elevator. Sometimes lots of people get on and off. But the elevator always seems to know how long to stop. The door doesn't close until the last person has gotten out or stepped inside.

Is the elevator thinking? Does it count the people? Not really—but it does "see" people coming and going. It has an electric eye!

At one side of the elevator there is a light that shines a beam across the open doorway. At the other side, an electric eye "sees" the beam of light. When nothing is in the doorway, the beam of light shines on the electric eye. This makes the electric eye send the door-opening machine a signal to close the door. But when people step in or out, they walk between the beam of light and the electric eye. This keeps the electric eye from sending the door-closing signal, so the door stays open.

The door stays open as long as people walk through the beam of light. When everyone is in or out, the beam of light shines on the electric eye again. Then the electric eye sends its signal. The door closes and the elevator glides up or down to another floor.

Lamp Number 9

In the year 1879, a few city streets were lit with electric lights—hot, glaring lights that could only be used outdoors. Thomas Edison thought electricity could light people's houses, too. But he knew that a different kind of light was needed.

Edison was already a successful inventor when he began working on the electric light, or *lamp*, as he called it. But the job wasn't easy, even for him. A great many attempts and errors, as well as a lot of plain hard work, went into this invention.

Tom Edison sat in his laboratory, watching an assistant light the gas lamps. The sight always bothered him. For years he had been convinced that electricity could be used to make light—a light as pleasant and soft as gas light, but without the bad smell or the open flame of burning gas.

But making an electric lamp was harder than he had thought. In fact, it was turning out to be more trouble than any invention he had ever worked on! He was using up glass bulbs as fast as his glassblower could make them. But no matter what shape the bulbs were, or how he arranged the wires inside the bulb, the lights never lasted long.

One of the big problems was the filament, the thin wire that gave off light inside the bulb. It had to be made of something that would glow—but not burn—when electricity ran through it.

Edison had tried dozens of different filaments, including wires made of rare metals. So far platinum seemed to work best. By winding a thin platinum wire into a tight coil, he made a filament that would give a bright light. And by pumping nearly all the air out of the glass bulb, he managed to keep the filament from burning up too quickly. But the platinum wire still got too hot. The only way to keep it from melting was to add a

switch that turned the lamp off every few minutes.

So the platinum-wire bulb just wasn't working. And platinum was expensive—over five dollars an ounce. Most people couldn't afford to buy an expensive lamp that burned only a few hours. The bulb would have to use a filament made from something cheaper and longer-lasting than platinum.

Edison began leafing back through the notebooks in which he wrote up his experiments. Maybe some of the materials he had tried before should be tried again. Carbon— what about carbon? A piece of carbon might work. But carbon burned very easily. He would have to pump as much air as possible out of the bulb, so that the carbon would glow without burning. And the carbon would have to be very thin, like a piece of wire.

Carbon crumbled easily, too. It would be hard to make the soft, black powder into a wire. But maybe he could mix the carbon with something else.

Edison hunted around the laboratory until he found a small lump of tar. He warmed the tar until it was soft, mixed in the carbon, and rolled it into a thin "wire."

The carbon gave good light—but only for an hour or two. And it was hard to make the "wire" thin enough and strong enough at the same time.

Edison called in Charles Batchelor, an

assistant who had especially steady and skillful hands. For days he and Batchelor rolled and squeezed mixtures of carbon and tar. But even Batchelor broke dozens of the thin "wires" before he could get them rolled and mounted in the lamps.

"There's got to be another way," Edison said to Batchelor, who was carefully trying to roll another filament. "If we could just burn a thin piece of something to make a thread of carbon. . . . Thread! Batch, get me a spool of thread!"

At once he and Batchelor set to work, shaping pieces of plain white cotton thread into a hairpin curve and baking them in the laboratory oven. While the threads were baking, Edison sent his glassblower an order for still more of the pear-shaped bulbs they needed. Then, after the blackened thread had cooled, Batchelor tried to fasten one of the thin pieces of carbon into one of the new glass bulbs.

Every piece broke! Again and again Edison and Batchelor baked threads. Eight times they managed to get a thread out of the oven and into one of the glass bulbs. But each time the thread broke before the lamp could be tested.

Batchelor's steady hands grew tired. But he managed to get the carbon thread into Lamp Number 9 without breaking it. Carefully, Edison and Batchelor pumped the air out of the bulb. Then they turned on the electric current and sealed the bulb.

Number 9 glowed with a soft light, like a small sun. And it kept on glowing! Hours later the bulb was still working. Edison increased the current. The lamp burned an hour longer before it broke. "Then cracked glass and busted," Edison wrote in his notes.

There were still problems to be solved, Edison knew. But he was on the right track—his idea had worked. Lamp Number 9 had given over half a day of light! If it could burn that long,

Edison was sure he could make an electric light that would burn even longer. And he had wonderful plans—plans for lighting houses, factories, streets, and even whole cities with glowing wires in small bulbs of glass.

Thomas Edison kept working—and he made his wonderful plans come true. A little more than a year after Lamp Number 9 was tested, one of his bulbs burned for 1,589 hours—over 66 days.

The light bulbs we use today have filaments made of a metal called tungsten (TUHNG stuhn) instead of a thin carbon thread. But in other ways they are very much like Lamp Number 9. And they are doing exactly what Edison thought they could do—lighting houses and factories, streets and cities all over the world!

Superlight!

It punches through steel. It carries complicated messages. It performs tiny, delicate operations. Anything that can do so many kinds of work should be magic. But this isn't magic—it's a special kind of light.

The light that can do these things is a laser (LAY zuhr) beam. A laser beam is made up of bunches of energy called photons, just like ordinary light. But the photons in a laser beam behave in an unusual way.

The photons in ordinary light are not all alike, and they don't all move together. They behave almost like people in a crowded street—dressed differently, going in all directions, and starting and stopping at different times.

But in laser light, all the photons are put to work in the same way. They are exactly the same color, so they all have the same amount of energy. They are given off at regular times, and they travel in one direction. They are almost like marchers in a parade—dressed in uniforms and moving in step down a narrow street.

With all the photons moving together, laser light can do things that ordinary light can't do. Laser light can create tremendous amounts of heat—enough heat to burn through heavy metal. It can be sent in a very narrow beam—so narrow it can drill a tiny hole in a diamond or treat a tiny spot in a patient's eye. And it can move steadily in a single direction—steadily enough to carry thousands of messages for telephones and TV shows. Laser light can even be used to find and guide satellites in space.

Round and flat

Your dog was chasing a big red ball when the picture was taken. The ball was round—but the one in the picture looks like a flat red circle. Why doesn't the ball in the picture look like the real ball?

Special pictures called holograms make things look real. When light shines through the film, you see the pictured thing from all sides.

When you look at something, you really see two different pictures. Your eyes are about three inches (7.5 centimeters) apart. So each eye gets a slightly different view. The two views blend into one picture that makes things look round or flat, far or near.

The camera works somewhat like your eye. But with one lens, it sees only one view. When you look at the picture, your eyes have nothing to blend. So a picture of something looks flat.

A special kind of camera has two lenses set a small distance apart. It takes two pictures at the same time. But each lens "sees" a slightly different view, so each picture is a little different. The pictures are put in a special viewer, so that you see one view with each eye. Then both pictures blend together. Whatever you look at seems round or flat, near or far.

With a laser beam, people can make special pictures called holograms (HOHL uh gramz). *Hologram* means something like "whole picture." And that's just what a hologram is—a picture that shows a whole thing.

The picture is taken with laser light instead of ordinary light. And it never gets printed on paper! The hologram can only be viewed by shining a beam of light through the film. The picture you see then looks completely real. You can even look over, under, and around the things that are in the picture.

Stand-out pictures

The pages in this book are flat and smooth. So are the pictures on the pages. But if you look at the picture pairs on the opposite page in a special way, the things in them will seem to stand out from the page. All you need is a small mirror and a little bit of patience.

Lay the picture page on a table, directly in front of you. Look at the first pair of pictures. Hold the mirror up to the right side of your nose and look into it with your right eye. Move the mirror until you can see the right-hand picture in it.

Now look at the left-hand picture with your left eye. Keep your right eye on the picture in the mirror, and tilt the mirror slowly to the left. With practice, you can make the two pictures slide together until they are perfectly matched. Then you will see one picture that looks "real."

Putting light to work

What's on TV tonight? Why, nothing but thousands of lines full of millions of spots of light. *That's* what makes up the program you are watching!

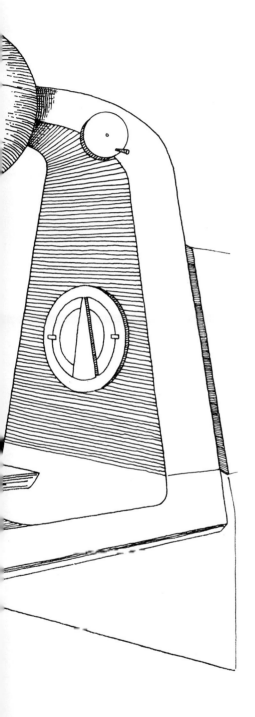

Part of a TV camera makes an electric copy of the scene. It changes bright and dark spots to strong and weak spots of electricity.

Then another part of the TV camera "reads" the spots. It zips across the scene in lines. But it "reads" much faster than people do. It turns a scene into more than five hundred lines—and it does this thirty times in a second!

As each line is read, strong and weak electric signals are sent from the TV station to your set. The signals make a part inside the TV set shoot electrons at the screen. The electrons zip across in lines, changing the strong and weak signals back into bright and dark spots. And there is your TV picture, in millions of spots of light.

You can smile for a TV camera, but don't bother smiling for an X-ray machine. It only takes pictures of what's *inside* you. It does this by shooting X rays through your body!

X rays are somewhat like ordinary light. But they pass right through your skin and all the soft parts of your body. Only hard or thick parts stop them.

So when an X-ray picture is taken, the X rays pass through most of you and hit the film. But the parts that stop the X rays cause a shadow. When the film is developed, it shows shadows of bones, teeth, or thick parts such as your heart.

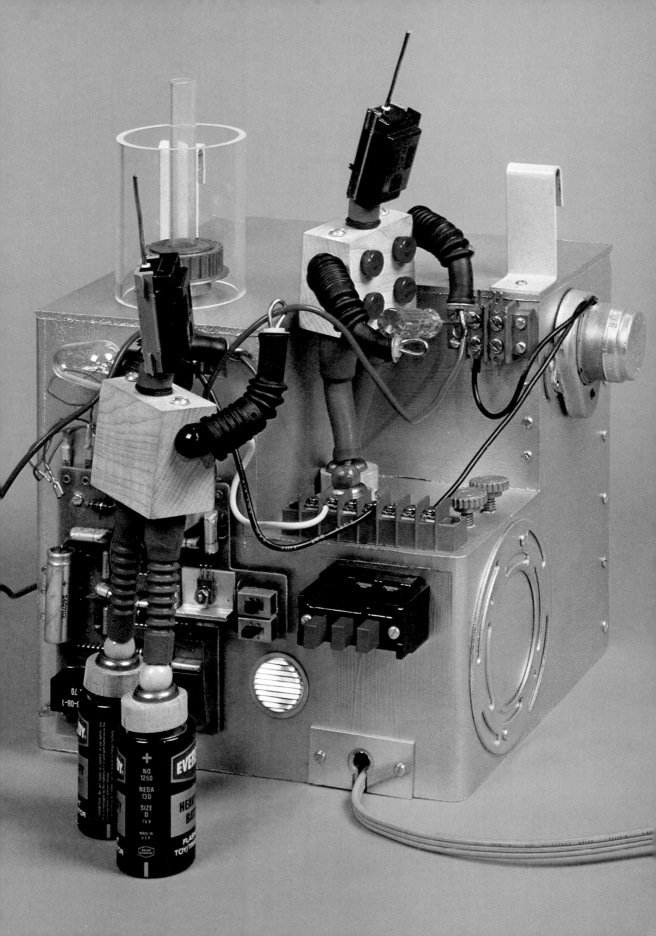

Currents and Sparks

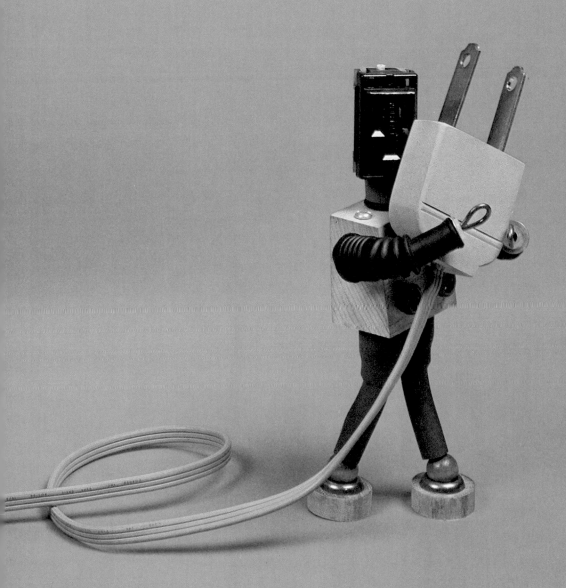

What is electricity?

When you turn on a light, ring a doorbell, or plug in a coffee pot, you start a parade—but it's a parade you can't see!

The parade is a parade of moving, pushing electrons (ih LEHK trahnz). The energy of the moving electrons is called electricity. It is what makes the light, the doorbell, and the coffee pot work.

All matter is made up of tiny bits called atoms. Every atom has a center, or nucleus (NOO klee uhs). The nucleus is surrounded by one or more spinning electrons.

In some kinds of matter, the electrons can move very easily. They can be pushed from atom to atom. As the electrons move, they push on other electrons and make those electrons move. They make a sort of "parade."

Each electron in the "parade" carries only a small amount of energy. And each electron travels only a short distance on each push. But inside a single wire there are millions and millions of electrons. So, when you press a button or turn a switch, the parade you start is a big one! Millions of electrons move through the wire, making a strong push that gets work done.

Making sparks fly

Do sparks fly when you pull your jacket off?
Do you get a crackling shock when you touch
a doorknob? These things happen because
you've been collecting electricity!

The sparks and crackles are static (STAT
ihk) electricity—electrons that pile up in one
place. On cool, dry days, you collect electrons
very easily. You actually scrape them loose
from things! When you walk across a rug, or
when your jacket rubs against you, the loose
electrons stick to your body.

The loose electrons can't flow through you
the way they flow through a wire. But they
can *jump* from you to a kind of material that
has fewer electrons. So, when you reach for
the doorknob or pull off your jacket, that's
exactly what happens. Then you hear the
crackle of electrons jumping from place to
place—and sometimes you feel it, too!

A moving electron show

Would you like to see the pull and push electrons make? You can do it with static electricity you collect on a balloon.

Blow up both balloons and tie strings to them. Rub one balloon with the cloth. Then touch the balloon to the cloth and let go of the string. What happens?

Rub *both* balloons with the cloth. Hang the balloons next to each other. What happens this time?

When you rub the balloons, they pick up electrons from the cloth. The balloons then have more electrons than the cloth.

When you put a balloon next to the cloth, the piled-up electrons on the balloon begin to move back to the cloth. They make a pull that sticks the balloon to the cloth.

But when you put the two balloons together, the piled-up electrons have nowhere to go. Both balloons have too many electrons, so they push each other away.

Materials

- balloons (2)
- string
- wool cloth

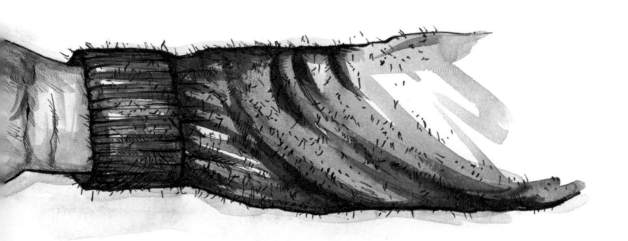

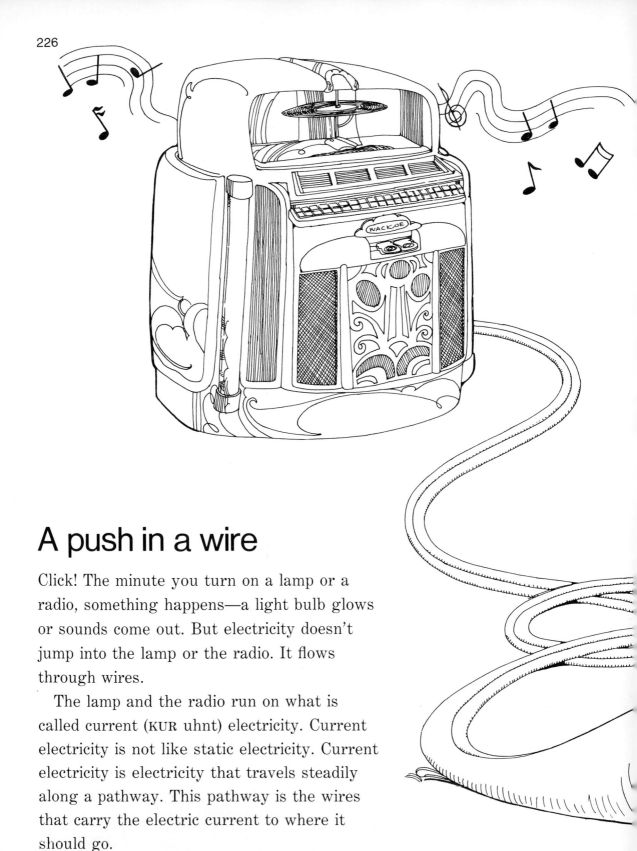

A push in a wire

Click! The minute you turn on a lamp or a radio, something happens—a light bulb glows or sounds come out. But electricity doesn't jump into the lamp or the radio. It flows through wires.

The lamp and the radio run on what is called current (KUR uhnt) electricity. Current electricity is not like static electricity. Current electricity is electricity that travels steadily along a pathway. This pathway is the wires that carry the electric current to where it should go.

The center of the wire is a metal, such as copper. Metals have electrons that are free to move about. So, the electrons can move along the metal.

The outside of the wire is made of rubber or plastic. The electrons in rubber or plastic are held tightly to their atoms. They can't move from one atom to another.

When the electric current is turned on, the metal part of the wire conducts (kuhn DUHKTS), or carries, the electricity. The electrons push along the wire from atom to atom, carrying electrical energy. But the plastic or rubber covering doesn't carry electricity. So, the rubber or plastic covering insulates (IN suh layts), or seals off, the wire. It keeps the moving electrons from leaving the path to your lamp or radio.

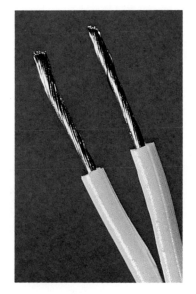

The metal part of the wire carries electricity. The rubber or plastic covering keeps the electric current from leaving the wire.

Current conductors

Materials

- bell wire (6 feet; 1.8 meters)
- dry cell (No. 6)
- flashlight bulb (1.5 volts)
- knife
- porcelain or plastic socket (small, for flashlight bulb)
- screwdriver

What kinds of materials will conduct, or carry, electricity? This safe conduction tester will help you find out.

Ask a grown-up to cut the wire in half, and then to cut one of the pieces in half again. Now scrape about an inch (2.5 centimeters) of the covering from the ends of the wires.

Attach the two short wires to the screws on the socket, as shown. Then connect one short wire to a post on the battery. Connect one end of the long wire to the other post.

Screw the bulb into the socket. Then touch the free ends of the short and long wires together. If the bulb lights up, your conduction tester is ready to use.

Find several kinds of material to test, such as aluminum foil, coins, a cork, an eraser, a glass, keys, paper, pins, plastic toys, and a wooden block. Touch the free ends of the bare wires to each sample. (Make sure the wires don't touch each other.) Does the bulb always light up?

Most metals are good conductors of electricity. An electric current passes through them easily. So the bulb lights up. But materials such as rubber, wood, and plastic are not good conductors. So when these things are used, the bulb on your conduction tester does not light up.

Are *all* metal things good conductors? Do any other materials conduct electricity? Test more samples to find out.

What makes the push?

Electricity is a push in a wire—the push of moving electrons. But what makes the electrons *start* to push through the wire? Where does electricity come from?

Electricity is made in a kind of "electricity factory" called a power plant. The special machine that makes electricity is called a generator (JEHN uh ray tuhr).

A generator uses a huge spinning magnet to make electrons move. The pull of the spinning magnet is strong enough to start electrons pushing in a wire.

The magnet is surrounded by a huge coil of tightly wound wire. When the magnet begins to spin, its pull starts millions of electrons pushing! This push makes a strong electric current in the coiled wire. The current is sent through other wires from the power plant to your home.

A generator makes electrical energy. But a generator uses energy, too. Running water, burning fuel, or nuclear energy runs the engines or other machines that make the huge magnets spin. So a generator actually is an energy-changing machine. It changes other kinds of energy into electrical energy— energy you can use.

Starting and stopping the push

You want your electric clock to run day and night. But you wouldn't want your doorbell ringing all the time! Things like doorbells, lamps, and radios work only when you turn them on.

Most things that run by electricity have a switch—a part that is used to turn the electric current on and off. The electric current moves along the wire and across the switch to another wire inside the bell, lamp, or radio. The switch is a "bridge" in the path the electricity follows.

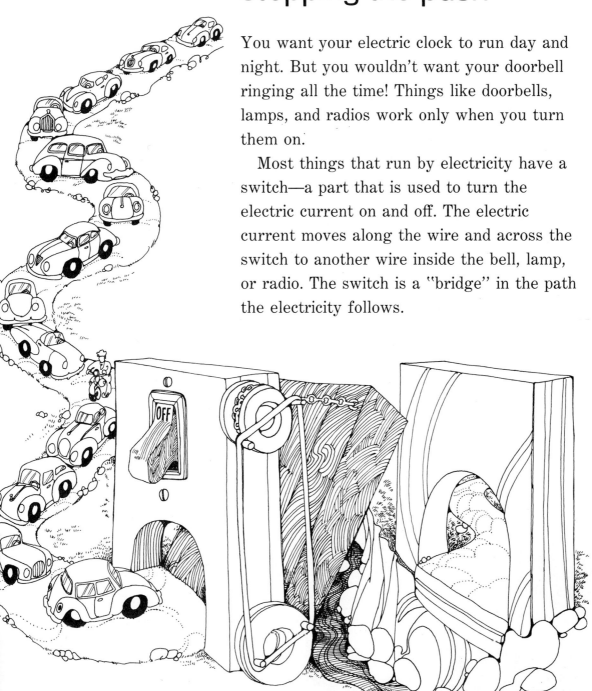

Inside the switch is a metal piece that moves when you turn the switch on and off. When you turn the switch *on*, the metal piece touches both wires. The "bridge" is down. The electricity coming into the switch can cross the "bridge" and keep traveling along the pathway.

But when you turn the switch *off*, the metal piece moves away from the wire. The "bridge" is up. Without the "bridge," the electric current can't cross the switch and follow the path. So, the electric current stops moving, and things stop working until you lower the "bridge" in the pathway by turning the switch on again.

Electricity traveling through the thin wire of a light bulb makes the bulb glow.

It's light!

When you turn on a lamp, electricity makes the bulb light up. But the whole bulb isn't really glowing. The part that gives light is a tiny wire inside the bulb.

The electricity you are using follows a path through a wire into the lamp. When the electricity reaches the bulb, it pushes in through the metal piece on the bottom. It travels around a wire path inside the bulb. Then it leaves the bulb again.

Part of the path through the bulb is a special filament (FIHL uh muhnt)—a very thin thread of coiled wire. Because the filament is very thin, the electrons traveling around the path can't pass through it easily. They push hard to get through the thin wire.

The push of the electrons makes the

When the wire in the bulb breaks, the electricity stops flowing. The bulb is "burned out."

molecules in the filament move faster and faster. The molecules get hotter and hotter as they speed up—so hot that the electrons in the molecules give off energy. The filament glows!

The filament in the light bulb is made of a special metal called tungsten (TUHNG stuhn). A tungsten wire can get very hot without burning or melting. But tungsten evaporates very slowly as it is heated—its molecules change to a gas and leave the wire. So, as the light bulb glows, the filament gets thinner and thinner.

After many hours of use, the filament breaks. The bulb is "burnt out." The electricity can't get across the break in the filament. Then you put in a new bulb. Now the electric current has a path to follow. The lamp lights up again.

It's hot!

When you use electricity to make toast, pop corn, iron clothes, or dry your hair, two things happen. Electricity makes a strong push in a wire—and the wire pushes back!

Electricity makes the toaster and other things heat up—much the way it makes a light bulb glow. The electricity travels into and out of these things on a pathway of wire.

Most of the wire in the pathway conducts electricity easily. The electrons in the wire are free to move, so the current pushes steadily along the wire. But inside these things, part of the pathway is made of a different kind of wire.

The wire in this part of the pathway is a different kind of metal—a kind of metal in which the electrons don't move very easily. Often the wire is very thin—and sometimes it is wound into a long, tight coil.

Instead of conducting electricity easily, this part of the pathway *resists* (rih ZIHSTS) the current. The electrons have to push hard to move through the wire.

The pushing electrons make the molecules in the wire speed up and bump against each other. The harder they bump and push, the hotter the wire gets. In a few minutes, all the bumping and pushing makes the wire hot. And the heat toasts the toast, pops the corn, smooths the clothes, or dries your wet hair.

The Lightning Rods

From *Ben and Me*
by Robert Lawson

Ben and Me is the story of a mouse named Amos who supposedly lived with the famous American leader and scientist, Benjamin Franklin. In this episode, Amos tells of Dr. Franklin's attempts to discover the nature of lightning. And in real life, Benjamin Franklin did prove that lightning is electricity.

. . . I observed that Ben was developing an unseemly interest in lightning. Every time a house or a tree was struck Ben was the first to reach the scene, questioning all who had been present as to how the bolt had looked, smelled or sounded, what sensations they had felt, and so on. Then he would go into a brown study that lasted for hours, occasionally murmuring, "I wonder, I wonder."

"Wonder what?" I asked finally. It was getting on my nerves.

"Why, if lightning and electricity are the same thing."

"To me they are," I said promptly. "They're both annoying, horrid, dangerous nuisances that should be let strictly alone."

"There you go again, Amos. No vision—no vision."

"All right," I said. "ALL RIGHT. And if they are the same and if you do prove it, then what?"

"Why then," he said, "why then, I shall go down in history as he who tamed the lightning, who—"

"If you have any notion of making a house-pet of this lightning," I said, "you can go down in history as anything you please. For myself, I will go down in the cellar—and stay there."

Two days later I was waked from my afternoon nap by a terrible clatter overhead. Investigation disclosed Ben seated on the roof busily hammering. He had fastened a whole collection of sharp-pointed iron rods to various parts of the housetop. There were two or three on each chimney and a series of them along the ridgepole. These were all connected by a tangle of wires and rods that ran down through the trapdoor into our room.

"You see, Amos," he explained, while connecting wires to various instruments, "the trouble with most people is that they lack the calm observation of the trained scientific mind. Time after time I have rushed to the scene of one of these lightning strokes and all I could gather from the bystanders was that they were 'terrible skeered.'

"Now by collecting a small amount of this so-called 'lightning' with the rods which you saw on the roof and conducting it through wires to these jars and instruments, we shall be able to investigate its nature and behavior with true scientific calm. We shall be able to settle forever the question which is puzzling all great minds, the question of whether or not lightning is electrical."

"It never has puzzled my mind," I said. "Left to myself I wouldn't give it a thought.

"Moreover," I continued, "you might as well leave out that 'we.' I resigned from these experiments a long time ago. Any observing that I do will be done in the cellar. And as the sky has clouded up rather threateningly I think I will retire there at once."

The storm must have been closer than I thought, for I had barely started for the door when there occurred a most horrifying flash of lightning, followed by a thunder-clap that shook the house to its foundations.

The shock threw me bodily into a large glass jar, luckily empty. This was really fortunate, for here I was able to observe all that went on, while the glass seemed to protect me from

the lightning flashes that now followed one another in rapid succession.

At the first flash the liquid in Ben's jars disappeared in a great burst of yellowish steam and the instruments bounced about wildly. As flash followed flash blue sparks ran up and down the wires, the brass andirons glowed as though dipped in phosphorus and streaks of fire shot from the candlesticks on the mantelpiece. The crashing thunder was, of course, continuous, jarring every loose object in the house.

There was now no doubt in my mind that lightning was electricity—in its most horrid and dangerous form.

In the confusion I had forgotten Ben. Now, looking about, I was astonished to find him nowhere in sight.

At this moment a large ball of blue fire emerged from the Franklin stove, rolled across the floor and descended the stairs, crackling and giving off a strange odor of sulphur. The unusually violent crash that followed brought a faint moan from the bed.

There I discovered Ben, or rather his feet, for they were the only part of him visible. The rest was covered by the bedclothes, while two pillows completely muffled his head.

At first I was alarmed, but as each succeeding crash brought an echoing moan and a violent trembling of the feet I realized that all that had befallen him was a severe case of fright.

Safe in my glass jar I thoroughly enjoyed the spectacle of Ben's terror as long as the storm raged.

As the last rumblings died away he cautiously raised the pillows and peered forth. He was a most amusing sight.

"And now, Dr. Franklin," I jeered as he sheepishly rose from the bed, "would you lend a bit of your calm, scientific study to getting me out of this jar? And by the way, what did you observe as to the true nature of lightning?"

"Do you know, Amos," he explained, "that first flash knocked off my glasses, and of course I see very poorly without them."

"So you replaced them with a couple of pillows," I said.

He never answered me—just started picking up the remains of his apparatus.

When, some time later, a scientific writer called them "Lightning Rods," naming Ben as their inventor, he refused to take the credit. This startling display of modesty surprised many people—but not me. I knew all about it.

Large electromagnets can lift heavy loads.
This one picks up and stacks big blocks
of crushed iron and steel in a junkyard.

An on-off magnet

Electricity can make light and heat. It can also make a magnet—one that you can turn on and off.

A magnet made with electricity is called an electromagnet (ih LEHK troh MAG niht). An electromagnet has two parts—a solid center, or core, and an outer covering made of many turns of wire. The core of an electromagnet is a piece of iron. By itself, iron is not a magnet. But it can be made to act like a magnet.

When an electric current runs through the wire that is wrapped around the iron core, the iron becomes a magnet. The iron gets its pull, or magnetism, from the moving electrons in the wire. As soon as the electric current is turned off, an electromagnet loses its magnetism.

Electromagnets make electric motors run. A motor has two sets of these magnets—an outer set that stays in place and an inner set that moves.

The inner set of electromagnets is attached to an axle—a rod that can spin. When the motor is turned on, the two sets of electromagnets push and pull against each other. That push makes the inner magnets move and set the axle spinning—and the spinning axle of the motor gives a push that makes machines work.

A pull from electricity

You can build your own electromagnet—and you can find ways to make your magnet stronger. This project will show you how.

Ask a grown-up to use the knife to scrape about an inch (2.5 centimeters) of the covering from each end of the wire. Beginning about a foot (30 cm) from one end of the wire, wind the wire evenly around one nail. Make as many turns as you can. Tape the wire at both ends of the nail to hold the wire in place.

Attach the bare ends of the wire to the two battery posts, as shown. Now test your magnet. How many paper clips can it pick up? Can it pick up heavier metal things?

Materials

- bell wire (6 feet; 1.8 meters)
- dry cell (No. 6)
- knife
- nails (2 large)
- paper clips (steel)
- tape

Making the pull stronger

Unhook the wire. Take the long end and wrap another layer of wire around the nail. Tape the ends of the wire in place and test your magnet again. What happens?

The magnet picks up a heavier load. Adding more wire makes the magnet stronger.

Now unwind the wire. Put the two nails together and wind a layer of wire around both nails. Test your new magnet. What happens this time?

The magnet with two nails picks up a heavier load than the magnet with one nail. Using a bigger core can make the magnet stronger, too.

What do you think will happen if you wind a second layer of wire around the two-nail magnet? Try it and see.

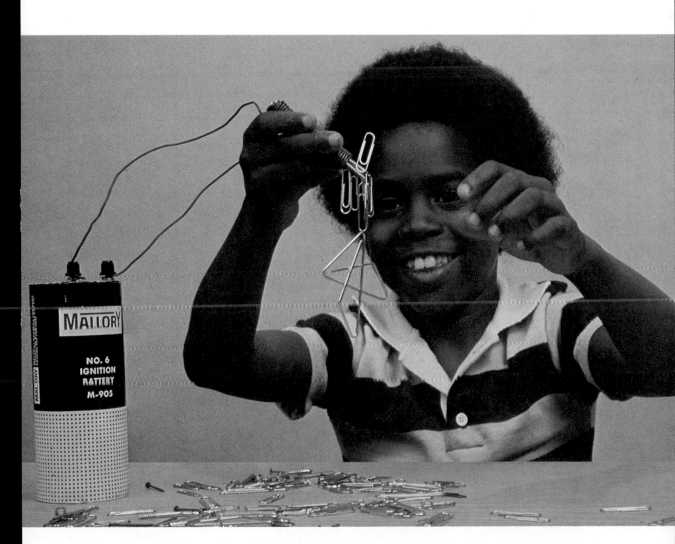

Making electricity safe

A light bulb uses only a little electricity. But electric stoves, refrigerators, and frying pans use as much electricity as dozens of light bulbs. Can you use too much electricity? What happens if you do?

Too much electricity traveling through a wire makes the wire hot—and a hot wire can be dangerous. It can start a fire. But a special safety switch in your house stops the electricity before the wire heats up.

One kind of safety switch is a fuse (FYOOZ). A fuse contains a thin metal bridge that the electric current crosses on its way through the wire.

If too much electricity is used at once, the metal in the bridge heats up. Before the wire can get too hot, the bridge melts and breaks. When this happens, we say that the fuse has "blown." The electric current is stopped and the wire stays cool.

Another kind of safety switch is a circuit

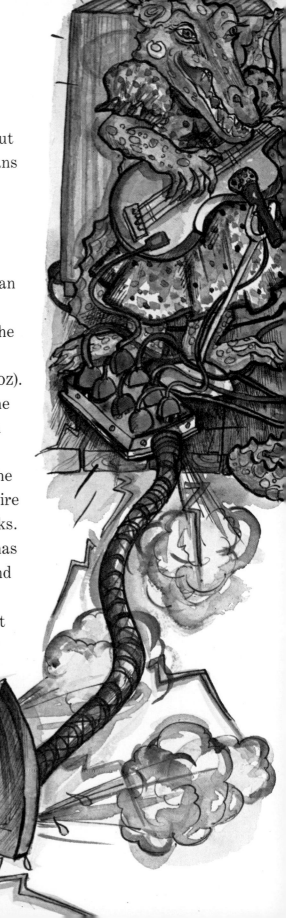

breaker (SUHR kiht BRAY kuhr). Instead of melting, a circuit breaker turns itself off.

One kind of circuit breaker contains an electromagnet. As more current is used, the electromagnet pulls harder. If too much current flows through the wire, the strong pull opens the switch. This stops the electric current before the wire can heat up.

Of course, the fuse can be replaced, or the circuit breaker can be reset, to turn the electricity on again. But first, some of the electric things you are using must be turned off. Then you will be sure you are not using too much electricity.

The metal bridge in a fuse is a safety switch. If too much electricity is used, the bridge breaks.

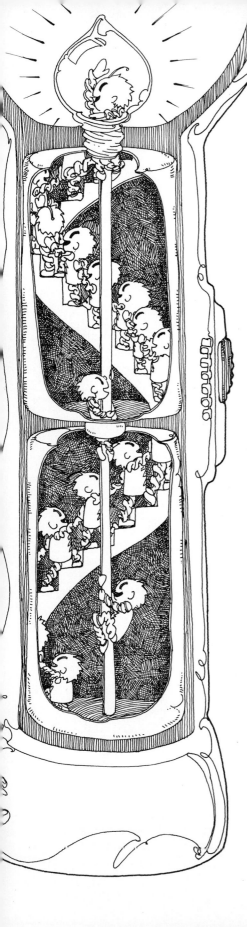

Packages of electricity

A flashlight runs on electricity—but you don't have to plug it in. It carries its electric current in a "package"—a battery.

A battery is made of layers of chemicals inside a metal can. When the flashlight is turned on, some of the chemicals in the battery break apart and eat away at the metal can. As this happens, some of the metal atoms leave the can and combine with the chemicals in the battery.

When the metal atoms move away from the can, they leave some of their electrons behind. So the can *gains* electrons. And as the chemicals inside the battery break apart, they *lose* electrons.

Soon, there are more electrons on the can than there are inside the battery. Then the extra electrons on the can begin to move out of the battery. They travel through the bulb and back into the middle of the battery, where electrons are scarce. The push of these electrons is the current that makes your flashlight shine.

This may make it seem that everything happens very slowly. But, as you know, it all takes place in an instant.

Lemon power

You can put your own "package" of chemicals together to make a battery. A tiny magnet—a compass needle—will show you when the electric current is flowing.

Ask a grown-up to use the knife to scrape about an inch (2.5 centimeters) of the covering from each end of the bell wire and all of the covering from the heavy wire. Beginning about a foot (30 cm) from one end, wrap twenty turns of wire around the compass.

Twist one of the bare ends of wire around the galvanized nail, just below the head. Twist the other end around the end of the heavy copper wire.

Squeeze or pound the lemon hard enough to break up some of the pulp inside. (Don't break the skin.) Then push the nail and the copper wire into the lemon, about an inch (2.5 cm) apart.

Watch the compass needle. Does it move? If it does, your lemon battery is making an electric current—and the current pushing through the wires around the compass is what makes the needle swing.

Materials

- bell wire (6 feet; 1.8 meters)
- compass
- heavy copper wire (No. 14, 2 inches; 5 centimeters)
- knife
- lemon
- nail (galvanized)

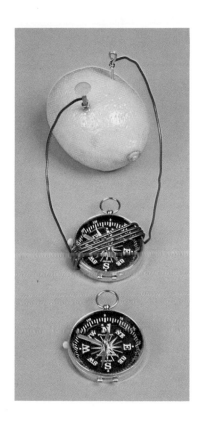

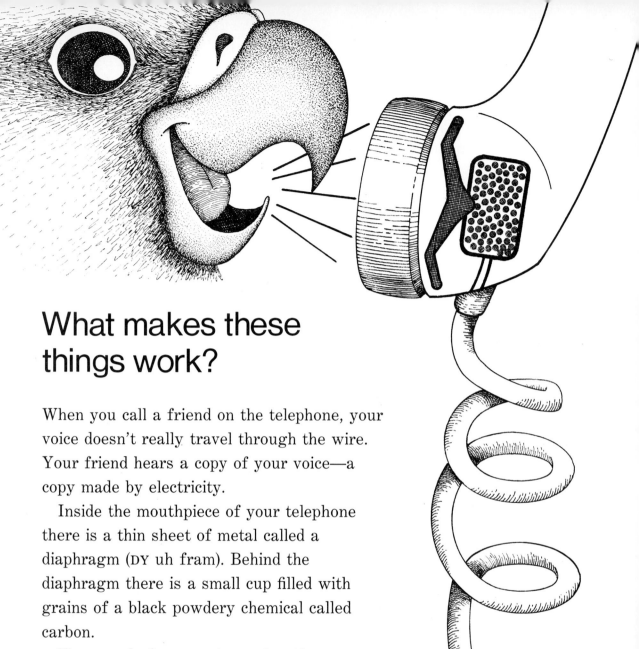

What makes these things work?

When you call a friend on the telephone, your voice doesn't really travel through the wire. Your friend hears a copy of your voice—a copy made by electricity.

Inside the mouthpiece of your telephone there is a thin sheet of metal called a diaphragm (DY uh fram). Behind the diaphragm there is a small cup filled with grains of a black powdery chemical called carbon.

The sound of your voice makes the diaphragm move in and out, or vibrate. As it vibrates, it presses against the carbon grains—sometimes very hard, sometimes very lightly.

Electricity passes through the carbon on its way through the telephone wire. When the carbon grains are squeezed together, the current travels through them easily. But when the grains are spread apart, only a little current can get through. So the vibrating diaphragm causes strong or weak pushes of electricity to travel through the telephone wire.

Inside the earpiece of your friend's telephone is an electromagnet. When the strong or weak pushes reach it, they cause this electromagnet to make strong or weak pulls on another diaphragm. These pulls make the diaphragm vibrate, producing sounds just like the ones you made. So your friend hears a copy of what you said—a copy made by electricity in a wire.

The music from a radio is an electric copy, too—a copy that travels by air.

Microphones and other equipment at the radio station change sounds into strong and weak electric signals. Then the signals are sent through the air from the station to your radio.

When you tune in the station, the signals go to an electromagnet in the radio speaker. The strong and weak pulls of the electromagnet cause parts of the speaker to vibrate and produce the sounds you hear.

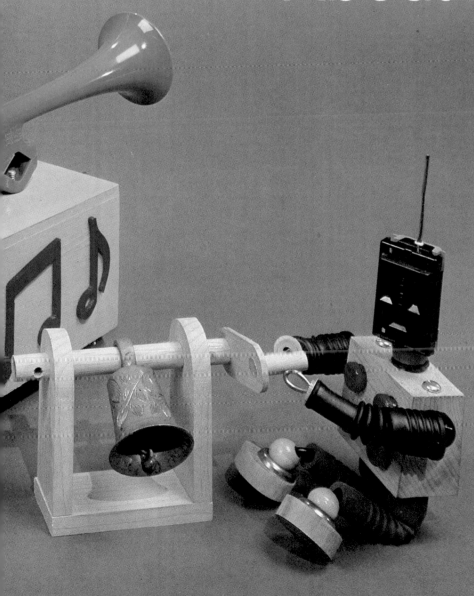

Hear All About It

What is sound?

Sound comes from just about everywhere—from friends talking, radios playing, jet planes roaring overhead. Even your breathing makes a tiny sound.

None of these sounds seem very much alike. But they are alike in one important way. They are made when something moves back and forth very quickly. These rapid back-and-forth movements are called vibrations (vy BRAY shuhnz). The vibrations travel through the air. When they reach our ears, we hear them as sounds.

When things vibrate, the back-and-forth movement is often too small and too fast for you to see. But sometimes you can feel the vibrations. Touch your throat with your fingertips when you are talking. Can you feel the movements when you speak? Vibrations inside your throat make the sounds you are saying.

Put your hand on the radio speaker when music is playing. Can you feel the beat? The speaker is vibrating. Its back-and-forth movements make the sounds that are the music you hear.

The vibrations you feel are energy—sound energy. Sound is making tiny pushes and pulls. When the vibrations stop, the sound stops, too. You don't hear another sound until things start vibrating again.

Now you hear it, now you don't

A ticking clock sounds loud when you put your ear close to it. But as you walk away, the ticking gets softer and softer—until you can't hear the clock at all. Why does the sound get softer?

The ticking you hear is made by the moving parts of the clock. These parts vibrate with a fast, back-and-forth motion. This back-and-forth motion is energy—tiny pushes and pulls. The pushes and pulls make the air around the clock move—they push the air molecules together into waves.

Sound waves are much like the waves you make when you drop a rock into a quiet pond. The waves in the water spread out in all directions. The sound waves from the clock also spread out in all directions. They move through the air to your ear, and you hear the ticking.

The sound waves are strongest where they are made—close to the vibrating clock. So when you stand next to the clock, the ticking you hear is loud.

But as the sound waves spread out through the air, they grow weaker and weaker, just as the waves in water do. So as you move away from the clock, the ticking gets softer.

By the time the sound waves have traveled across the room, the air is hardly moving at all. The pushes and pulls are too tiny for your ears to pick up—so you no longer hear the sound of the ticking clock.

Sound gets around

A swimming fish seems to glide through the water without making a sound. But it doesn't swim as quietly as you think! Divers swimming underwater hear a loud *crack* when a large fish flips its tail and darts away.

Most of the everyday sounds we hear travel through air. But sound waves travel through liquids and solids, too. Things like water, wood, and even the earth can conduct, or carry, the vibrations.

The molecules of liquids and solids are closer together than the molecules in air. And in some liquids and solids, the molecules are "springy"—when they are pushed, they bounce back, like a stretched rubber band.

These kinds of molecules vibrate easily
when a sound wave pushes them—and they
make other nearby molecules vibrate, too. So
in a solid or liquid with "springy" molecules,
sound travels fast—even faster than it
travels through air.

A loud sound takes about five seconds to
reach you if it travels a mile (1.6 kilometers)
through air. But under water, the same sound
reaches you in a little more than a second.
And a sound wave zips through a mile (1.6
km) of iron wire in about a third of a
second—almost fifteen times faster than it
travels through air.

Make a tin-can telephone

Materials

- hammer
- nails (3 small)
- thread (heavy duty—
  12 feet; 3.6 meters)
- tin cans (2)

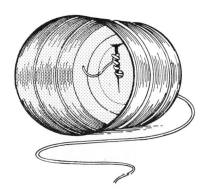

This telephone doesn't need electricity to work. A piece of thread carries the sound of your voice.

Have a grown-up use the hammer and one nail to punch a small hole in the center of the bottom of each can. Push the ends of the thread through the holes, from the outside to the inside, of each can.

Tie each end of the thread to a nail. Pull the thread until the nail touches the bottom of the can. Your "telephone" is ready to use.

Give a friend one of the cans. Stand far enough apart to stretch the thread tightly.

Talk softly into your end of the "telephone" while your friend holds the other can to one ear. Then have your friend talk while you listen.

When you talk, your voice makes the bottom of the can vibrate. The vibrations are conducted through the tight thread. When they reach the other end of the thread, they make the bottom of the second can vibrate— and your friend hears what you say.

You can make a "party line," too. Push a piece of thread through a third tin can. Tie the end to a nail. Then tie the other end of the thread to the middle of the first piece of thread. When the joined threads are stretched into a Y shape, you and your friends can have a three-way conversation.

High and low

Zzzeee goes the tiny mosquito as it zips past your ear. *HROOM* growls a big truck as it rumbles by on the road. The sound the mosquito makes is much higher than the sound of the truck. Why are the sounds different?

When something vibrates, sound travels outward from it in waves. Each vibration—each complete back-and-forth motion—makes a single wave. The faster something vibrates, the more waves it makes.

A mosquito makes high-pitched sounds because its wings vibrate very fast—about a thousand times a second. So every second, a thousand sound waves travel through the air—and you hear a high-pitched *zzzeee*.

A truck makes low-pitched sounds because the heavy metal parts vibrate slowly. The slow vibrations make only a few sound waves every second—the low rumble that you hear.

The number of times a sound wave vibrates in a second is called the frequency (FREE kwuhn see) of the sound. The higher the frequency is, the higher the sound you hear.

Most people can hear sounds with frequencies about twenty times greater than a mosquito's whine. And some animals can make and hear even higher sounds—sounds that people can't hear at all.

Sounds from moving things

Have you ever noticed a change in the "whistle" a train makes as it rushes by? If you stand by the tracks while the train is passing, the sound gets higher and then lower as the train goes by you.

Actually, the whistle makes the same sound all the time. The sound seems to change because the train is passing you.

The sound fans out in all directions from the train. But because the train is moving, each sound wave starts a little ahead of where the last one started. This makes the sound waves ahead of the train bunch up. Thus, more of the waves reach your ear every second. And the more waves that reach your ear in a second, the higher the sound.

But behind the train, the waves are spread apart. As the train speeds away, fewer waves reach your ear each second—so the sound gets lower.

A boom from moving air

Did you ever hear an earth-shaking, window-rattling crash of thunder on a clear, sunny day? It wasn't really thunder you heard. It was a sonic (SAHN ihk) boom—a sound made by something traveling *faster* than sound.

Anything that moves through the air—an airplane, a bird, or even a ball—pushes on the air ahead of it. It makes waves.

Most things never catch up with the waves they make. But some jet planes do. Supersonic (soo puhr SAHN ihk) planes can fly faster than sound travels. When they fly this fast, they slam into the waves of air they have made. This creates a tremendous air wave called a shock wave.

The shock wave spreads out behind the plane in a funnel shape. Traveling at the speed of sound, it crashes into the air and the ground around you. And this makes the sonic boom—the "thunder" you hear.

Hello . . . hello . . . hello

I met a man I could not see.
But I know he lives not far from me
Out past the lake, and up the hill,
For when the wind and the birds are still,
I stand alone and call "COME OUT!"
And down from the hill I hear him shout:
"OUT! OUT! OUT! OUT! OUT! OUT! OUT! OUT!"

—Well, it *starts* as a shout, as I think you see,
But gets small, and then smaller, then small as can be.
But you can't hear the smallest he knows how to say,
For it jumps up the hill and goes far far away
Till it dims into nothing and fades into sky.
And you still *seem* to hear it, far out and up high,
Till little by little you hear it grow still,
And you'd say there was no one up there on the hill.

But you know that there is. And he's someone you know.
And his name is— That's right! He is MR. ECHO.

I Met a Man I Could Not See
by John Ciardi

What happens when you shout a big "hello"
near a mountain, between tall buildings, or in
a large, empty hall or gym? Well, you may
hear an echo—another "hello" just like the
one you said.

Sound bounces off hard, smooth things the same way a ball bounces off a wall. The echo of your "hello" is reflected sound—sound that bounces back to you.

Why don't you always hear echoes? It depends on how far the sound goes before it bounces. In a small room, the sound you make travels only a short distance before it bounces. It comes back so fast that it seems like part of what you are saying.

But in a very large room, the sound travels a while before it bounces back. By the time the sound comes back, you have finished speaking. So you hear the sound a second time.

You can even hear the sound you make again, and again, and again. For example, if you shout between two tall buildings, the sound can bounce back and forth between the walls. When that happens, the sound is reflected back to you from more than one spot. You hear "hello . . . hello . . . hello . . ." from each reflected sound—until the sound dies out and the echoes stop.

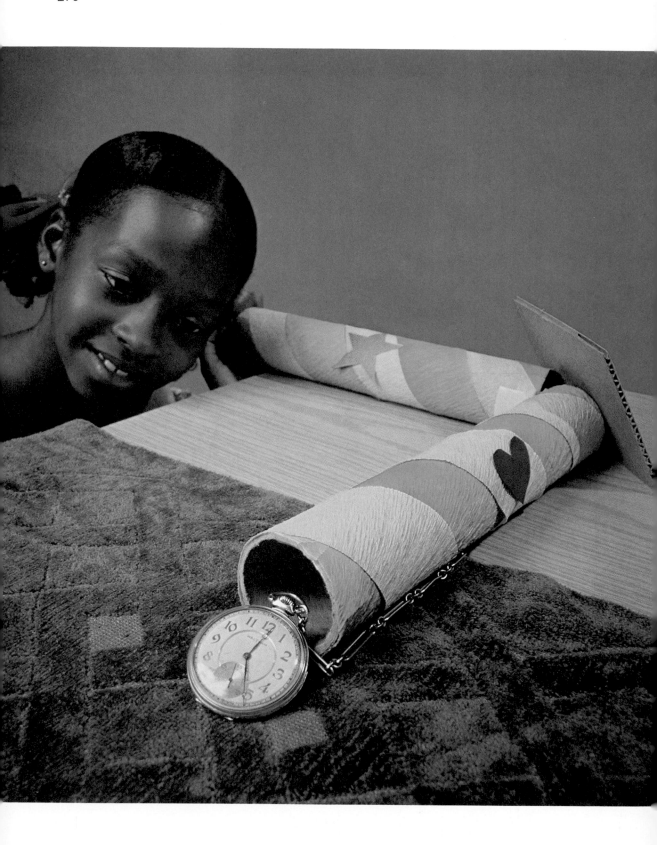

Making sound bounce

Sound waves bounce off hard surfaces such as walls and floors and ceilings. Here is a way you can prove this by making sound waves bounce around a corner.

Save the cardboard tubes from two rolls of paper towels. Fasten the tubes together with a piece of tape, as shown.

Arrange the tubes so that they form a corner. Place a folded towel at the free end of one of the tubes. Then lay the watch on the towel. Put your ear close to the free end of the second tube. Can you hear the watch ticking? No? Try it another way.

Hold the piece of cardboard in a slanted position across the open space between the tubes. Now put your ear close to the second tube. What happens this time? Now you can hear the ticking. Do you know why?

The sound waves made by the ticking watch travel through the first tube. But when the space between the tubes is open, the sound waves simply go out the open end. There is no way for them to get into the second tube.

When you place the cardboard across the open space, the sound waves bounce off the cardboard and into the second tube. The second tube carries the sound to your ear, and you hear the watch ticking. And that's how you can make sound go around a corner.

Materials

- cardboard
- cardboard tubes (2, same size)
- transparent tape
- towel
- watch (wind-up)

Music to your ears

What is music? It's making sounds you like—and putting the sounds together in different ways. You use the sounds to make a "design" you can hear, the same way you use a pencil or crayons to make a design you can see.

The design you make can be a beat, or rhythm (RIHTH uhm). It can be a tune you play or sing. And it can be the way different notes sound when you put them together.

You can make music with your voice, your tapping feet, and your clapping hands. Or you can use a musical instrument (IHN struh muhnt)—a special sound-maker. With musical instruments, you can make different kinds of sounds—high and low, loud and soft, short and long.

There are dozens of musical instruments
you can learn to play, each with its own
special sound. But all of these instruments
make sounds in only a few ways. So you can
think of each instrument as a member of a
family—a group that makes sounds in the
same way.

Percussion (puhr KUHSH uhn) instruments
are one family. They have parts that you hit
to make sounds. Another family, the stringed
instruments, has strings that you play. Two
families, the woodwinds and the brass
instruments, have tubes you blow into. And a
few instruments belong to very small families
that have special ways of making sounds.

Boom and bong

Tap a pencil against an empty box. It doesn't play a tune, but it does make a sound. One family of instruments makes sounds in the same way—you use something to hit, or strike, them. The instruments in this family are called percussion instruments. The word *percussion* means "striking."

A drum is a percussion instrument. It has a thin piece of material, called a *drumhead*, stretched over something hollow, like a can. When you strike the drumhead with a stick or your hand, the stretched material vibrates. This makes the air around the drum vibrate. It also makes the air *inside* the drum vibrate. The vibrations inside the drum bounce back and forth, somewhat like an echo. They make the sound stronger. Instead of a light tapping, you hear a loud *rat-tat-tat* or *boom-boom-boom*.

You can't play a tune on most drums, because they make only one kind of sound. But kettledrums, or timpani (TIHM puh nee), can make several different sounds. When the drumheads are tight, they vibrate fast and make a higher sound. When the drumheads are loose, they make a lower sound. So the drumheads are tightened and loosened to play a "tune."

A xylophone (ZY luh fohn), a glockenspiel (GLAHK uhn speel), and a marimba (muh RIHM

A drum has a tightly stretched covering called a drumhead. When you beat the drum, the drumhead vibrates and makes the sound you hear.

buh) are other percussion instruments that can be used to play tunes. Each one has bars of different lengths that make different sounds when you hit them. The short bars vibrate faster and make higher sounds than the long bars.

Cymbals (SIHM buhlz) are percussion instruments, too. They make a loud, clashing sound when you hit them together.

To play a violin, you rub the strings with a bow. The strings vibrate and make the sounds.

Singing strings

Can you make a string sing? You certainly can. When you play a stringed instrument, that's exactly what you do. Rubbing or plucking the tightly stretched strings makes them vibrate and produce sounds.

A violin has strings that make music when you rub them with a bow (BOH)—a wooden stick with horsehair stretched from one end to the other. When the bow is rubbed across the violin strings, it makes the strings vibrate. This makes the sound.

The strings are stretched over a thin wooden bridge on top of the violin. As the strings vibrate, they make the bridge vibrate. And the vibrating bridge makes the rest of the violin vibrate, too. All these vibrations make the full, rich violin sounds you hear.

You can make the sounds higher or lower by pressing down on the strings in different places. Pressing on the string changes the length of the part that vibrates. The shorter the vibrating part, the faster it moves and the higher the note sounds.

A viola (vee OH luh), a violoncello (VEE uh lahn CHEHL oh), and a double bass (DUHB uhl BAYS) are bigger relatives of the violin. Their larger bodies and longer, heavier strings make deeper sounds.

Some stringed instruments are played without a bow. You pluck the strings with your fingers, or with a thin, hard pick, to make them vibrate. A harp has short and long strings for the high and low sounds. On instruments such as the guitar, the strings are different thicknesses, but the same length. To make high notes, you shorten the strings by pressing them as you play.

"Wind" songs

Whistling can be music—you can make a tune with air you blow through your lips. Many musical instruments make sounds in the same way—with a stream of vibrating air.

A flute is one of these instruments. It belongs to the woodwind family. Not all woodwinds are made of wood, but they are all played with "wind"—your breath.

The flute has a mouthpiece with a small hole. When air is blown across the hole, it bounces against the edge. This makes the air in the flute begin to vibrate. The vibrations inside the tube create sound waves—and these make the music you hear.

To make higher and lower sounds, you press keys that open "windows" for the air.

The air inside a flute vibrates when you blow across the mouthpiece. The vibrating air makes a whistling sound.

For higher sounds, you open the holes close to the mouthpiece. The vibrations travel only a short distance down the tube to reach a "window," so a short sound wave is formed. For lower notes, you open holes farther down the tube. The vibrations travel farther to reach a "window," and longer waves are formed.

The piccolo (PIHK uh loh) is really a small flute—its name, in Italian, means "little." The short tube gives it a high, sharp sound.

The clarinet (klar uh NEHT), the oboe (OH boh), and the bassoon (buh SOON) have a mouthpiece with one or two thin, flat pieces called reeds attached. Blowing makes the reeds vibrate as the air passes over them. The vibrating reeds make the air vibrate, and the sound is carried to your ears.

Musical brass

Where does the loud, sharp sound of a trumpet come from? It all starts with a tiny "buzz"—a vibration very much like the one you make when you hum.

When you play a trumpet, your lips buzz against the mouthpiece. This starts the vibrations that make the sounds.

A trumpet belongs to the family of brass instruments. It makes music when you blow into the mouthpiece in a special way. You tighten your lips and make them vibrate against the cup-shaped mouthpiece as you blow. This makes the air in the trumpet vibrate, and you hear a sound. By changing the shape of your lips, you can make the air vibrate faster or slower, and make a higher or lower sound.

You can also change the sound by making it travel farther. A trumpet has several loops of tube that are closed off most of the time. Pressing a button opens a valve, or doorway, in a loop. When vibrations travel through one or more extra loops, they make a lower sound than if the valves were all left closed.

The cornet (kawr NEHT) sounds very much like a trumpet. The French horn (FREHNCH HAWRN) and the tuba (TOO buh) have longer, wider tubes. So the vibrations traveling inside the tubes make much longer waves. These waves produce much lower sounds.

One kind of brass instrument has no valves at all. To make high or low notes on a slide trombone (trahm BOHN), you actually make the tube shorter or longer! You push or pull on a U-shaped piece of tube that slides in and out of the trombone. The shorter you make the tube, the shorter you make the sound wave—and the higher you make the sound of the note you play.

Tiny hammers inside the piano hit the strings when you play. The vibrating strings make the sounds.

Hammers and strings

Have you ever made music with hammers? If you play the piano, you have. Small hammers hitting the wire strings make the sounds you hear.

The strings are different sizes. Long, thick strings that vibrate slowly make the low sounds. And short, thin strings that vibrate very quickly make the high sounds.

When you press down a piano key, two things happen. A small cushion swings out of the way so the strings for that key can vibrate. At the same time, the key pushes a lever. This lever swings the hammer against the strings.

If you hold the key down, the piano strings keep vibrating and the sound dies away slowly. But if you take your finger off the key, the cushion drops back onto the strings. The vibrations stop—and so does the sound you made.

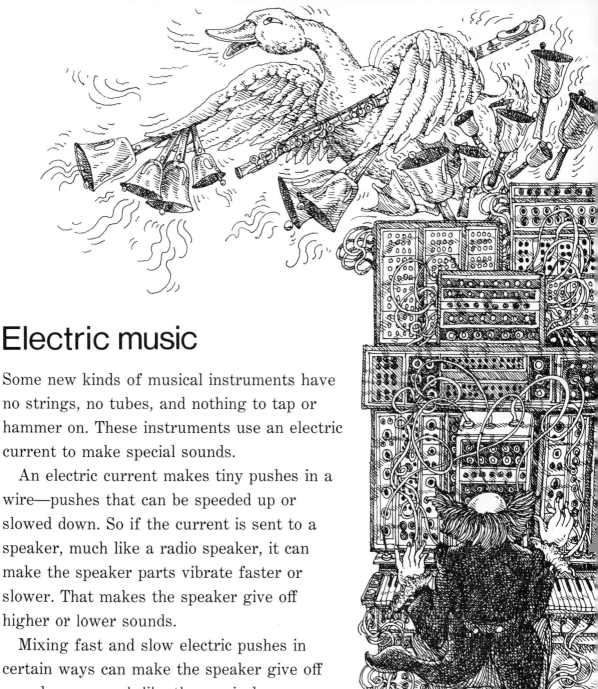

Electric music

Some new kinds of musical instruments have no strings, no tubes, and nothing to tap or hammer on. These instruments use an electric current to make special sounds.

An electric current makes tiny pushes in a wire—pushes that can be speeded up or slowed down. So if the current is sent to a speaker, much like a radio speaker, it can make the speaker parts vibrate faster or slower. That makes the speaker give off higher or lower sounds.

Mixing fast and slow electric pushes in certain ways can make the speaker give off sounds very much like the musical instruments you know. Or it can make the speaker vibrate in strange ways and create sounds that have never been made before. So the electric music you hear may sound like a single flute, a room full of bells, or even a giant duck—or all of them together!

Make your own music

Tap, plink, tweet, and *tootle.* Here are four simple instruments you and your friends can make. Each instrument belongs to a big family—it has lots of "relatives" that make music in the same way.

Tin-can bongos

Materials

- coffee cans (1 large, 1 small)
- plastic lids for cans
- masking tape

Bongo drums are percussion instruments that come in sets of two. Each drum makes a different tone when you tap it.

Snap the lids onto the cans. Make sure both lids fit tightly. Turn the cans upside down and stand them on a tabletop or other flat surface.

Have a friend hold the cans while you wind two or three layers of tape around them to

hold them together. Then turn the cans right side up. Your bongo drums are ready to play.

One drum is shorter than the other—so, of course, your bongos won't stand up. You sit on a chair or stool and hold them between your knees to play them.

Tap each drum with your fingertips. The smaller drum vibrates faster and gives out a higher sound than the larger one. You can use both hands to tap out a catchy rhythm with high and low sounds.

Rubber-band strummer

The "string" in this stringed instrument is a rubber band. You strum different parts of it to make different sounds.

Materials

- book
- paper cup
- rubber band

Place the paper cup on the book, with the open end up. Stretch the rubber band the long way around the book and over the cup.

Slide the cup close to one end of the book. Strum the part of the rubber band that goes across the open cup. Then strum the stretched part on each side of the cup. Do you hear three different sounds?

To "tune" your strummer, keep moving the cup as you strum the rubber band. The shorter and tighter you make one part of the rubber band, the higher the sound will be. Keep trying until you hear three notes that sound good together. Then use your strummer to play a three-note tune.

Soda-straw clarinet

This little instrument works very much like a real woodwind. The "reed" is one end of the straw.

Pinch one end of a soda straw to flatten it. The pinched part should be about as wide as your thumb. Trim the corners of the pinched part, as shown.

Put the pinched end of the straw into your mouth. Close your lips around the straw and blow hard. With a little practice, you should hear a low, loud sound, like the sound of a horn.

Now use the needle to punch five holes in the straw. The holes should be about an inch (2.5 cm) apart. Cut around each hole with small, sharp scissors to make it wider. Hold the straw in both hands and cover all the holes with your fingers. Now blow through the straw. You should hear the same note you heard before.

Beginning with the bottom hole, uncover the holes one by one. Each hole you uncover will make your clarinet play a higher sound.

Materials

- drinking straw (paper)
- needle
- ruler
- scissors

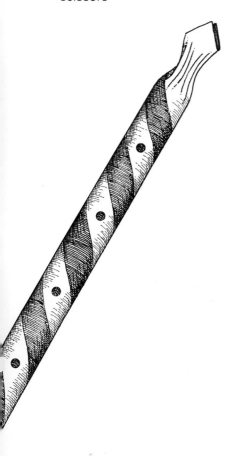

Bottle trombone

A bottle of water is the slide that makes this "trombone" play higher and lower.

Find a bottle that is almost as long as the straw you use. Rinse the bottle clean and fill it three-quarters full with water.

Materials

- bottle (plastic)
- drinking straw
- water

Stick the straw into the water. Holding the
straw in one hand and the bottle in the other,
blow a thin stream of air *across* the top of the
straw. You should hear a soft, whistling
sound made by the vibrating air in the straw.

Now move the bottle up and down as you
blow through the straw. When most of the
straw is *in* the water, only a short part of the
tube is filled with vibrating air. Blowing the
"trombone" makes a high sound. When most
of the straw is *out* of water, the air-filled
part of the tube is longer and you get a lower
sound.

With a little practice, you can learn to move
the bottle up and down to play a tune.

Singing and speaking

When you sing, *you're* a musical instrument—and when you speak, you're not. Singing and speaking are different, even though you make the sounds in almost the same way.

You sing and speak by making a part of your throat vibrate. The vibrations come from a pair of small, stretchy bands called vocal cords (VOH kuhl KAWRDS).

When you are not speaking or singing, the vocal cords are loose and relaxed, like an unstretched rubber band. Your breath goes in and out between the vocal cords without making them vibrate.

When you begin to speak, you use small muscles in your throat to pull the vocal cords tight. The air you breathe out pushes on the vocal cords and makes them vibrate. This vibration makes the sounds you hear—and you make the sounds into words by the way you move your tongue and lips.

When you sing, you make your vocal cords vibrate in the same way—but you change the speed at which they vibrate. To sing high, you tighten your vocal cords. This makes them vibrate faster. And to sing low, you loosen your vocal cords. This slows down the vibrations. So your vocal cords vibrate at exactly the right frequency, or rate of speed, for each sound—and your voice makes music.

Rattle and roar

Rattling trucks, roaring jets, squeaking chalk, and creaking doors don't make music. They make sounds we don't want to hear. These unwanted sounds are called noise.

Noise is hard to stop. Like other sounds, it travels through air and through solid things—even walls. And it bounces off floors, ceilings, or any smooth, hard surface. This makes noisy places even noisier!

But some materials actually "soak up" noise. They absorb sound waves and keep them from traveling. These materials are called insulators (IHN suh LAY tuhrz) because they are sound-stoppers.

Inside a building, rugs and curtains soak up sound. The soft threads and tiny air

Noisy airplane engines don't bother this airport worker. He wears insulated earmuffs that soak up the sound.

spaces in the material help trap the vibrations. Special ceiling tile can trap sound vibrations, too. The tile is full of tiny holes, like a sponge. When sound waves strike the tile, they bounce around inside the holes until they get weaker and die away.

Walls filled with insulators absorb sound in the same way. A thick, spongy layer inside the wall traps vibrations and keeps most of the sound from passing through.

People who work with airplanes and other heavy machines can't use rugs, curtains, or special walls and ceilings to soak up the sound—so they *wear* their insulators! Special helmets and earmuffs cover their ears while they are working. The sound-absorbing material shuts out most of the noise that could bother them or hurt their ears.

"Seeing" with your ears

When a friend calls your name across the playground, do you know which way to look? Usually you do—your ears tell you.

The outer part of your ear traps sound waves and funnels them into your ear. There the sound waves hit a thin, stretchy part called the eardrum. They make the eardrum vibrate and send a message to a nerve deep in your ear. The message travels up the nerve to your brain—and you hear.

Your ears are about six inches apart, so each ear hears sounds in a slightly different way. The ear that is closer to a sound hears it a little sooner and a little more loudly. It receives each part of the wave just a little before the other ear does.

These differences are very tiny—but they are big enough to tell you where the sounds

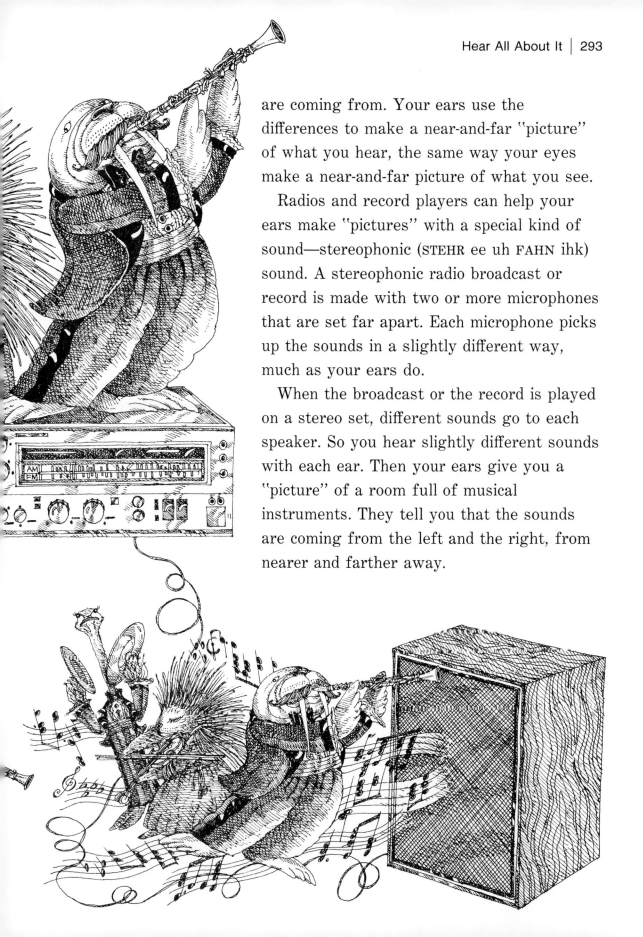

are coming from. Your ears use the differences to make a near-and-far "picture" of what you hear, the same way your eyes make a near-and-far picture of what you see.

Radios and record players can help your ears make "pictures" with a special kind of sound—stereophonic (STEHR ee uh FAHN ihk) sound. A stereophonic radio broadcast or record is made with two or more microphones that are set far apart. Each microphone picks up the sounds in a slightly different way, much as your ears do.

When the broadcast or the record is played on a stereo set, different sounds go to each speaker. So you hear slightly different sounds with each ear. Then your ears give you a "picture" of a room full of musical instruments. They tell you that the sounds are coming from the left and the right, from nearer and farther away.

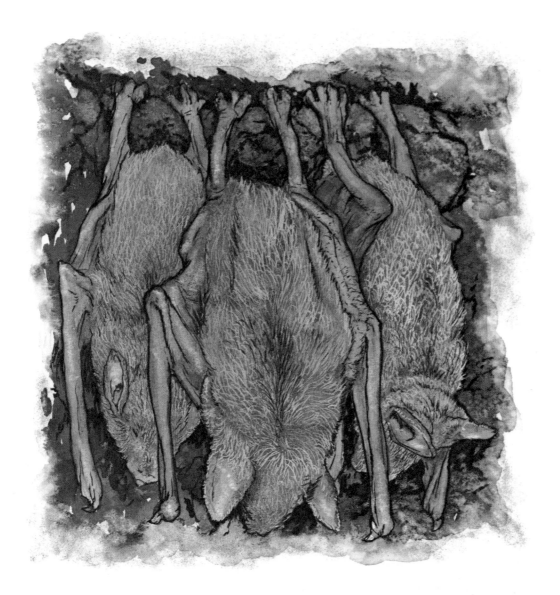

Hunter in the Darkness

In a cave in Texas, a furry, gray bat hung head downward, his eyes closed. The curved, sharp claws on his toes clung to the rough rock of the cave's ceiling. Even though he slept, the bat could not fall.

Pressing against him on all sides, hanging

asleep as he was, were other bats. The walls
and ceiling of the cave were a forest of furry
bodies. Even had there been light in the cave,
not a bit of rock could have been seen. It was
completely covered by tens of millions of
bats! They stretched from just within the
cave's entrance to deep down inside. In the
dark depths of the cave, the entrance was
only a small circle of light, far in the
distance.

Outside the cave it was late afternoon. The
sky was bright and blue, although the sun
was low.

The bat's eyes opened. He began to clean
himself. He licked the smooth skin on the
inside of his wings. Then he combed the fur
on his body with the claws of one foot. After
a time, he let himself drop from his perch. As
he fell, he opened his wings and flew toward
the cave entrance.

As he flew, the bat held his mouth open, his
lips pushed into the shape of a horn. From his
throat came a constant series of squeaking
noises. Each squeak made the air vibrate
more than thirty thousand times a second.
These squeaks couldn't have been heard by a
human—they were too high. For, people
cannot hear any sound that vibrates the air
more than twenty thousand times a second.

The sound waves sped out of the bat's open
mouth. They moved through the air in a
straight line ahead of him. Whenever they

struck anything—a part of the cave, or
another bat—they bounced straight back. The
bat's big ears picked up the returning sound
waves. The vibrations made the bat's
eardrums vibrate and send a message to his
brain. And his brain told him instantly where
and how far away the object was.

The bat joined many others near the
entrance of the cave. They grew more excited
as evening approached. Squeaks and the noise
of many flapping wings filled the cave. The
sound became as loud as the noise of a fast-
moving railroad train!

Soon, even though the sky was still bright,
millions of bats began to stream out of the cave
entrance. To anyone watching from a distance,

it would have looked like a thick cloud of smoke
pouring up out of the cave.

With many of the others, the bat headed for
a nearby pond. Swooping down, he scooped up
a mouthful of water. Then, with his thirst
quenched, he wheeled away through the sky
to find food.

It was dusk by now, and the sky was quickly
getting dark. This didn't matter a bit to the
bat. From his open mouth came one burst of
sound vibrations after another. These shot out
ahead of him. Each burst lasted only a fraction
of a second. After each, the bat listened for a
quick moment. From echoes that came back,
he could "see" anything ahead of him, from a
thick telephone pole to a tiny winged insect.

And, it was tiny flying insects the bat was hunting for. Any insect that flew through the bat's stream of vibrations, even up to eleven and a half feet (3.5 meters) away, sent an echo bouncing back. At once, the bat knew exactly where the insect was and in what direction it was moving. In less than a *second*, he had scooped it up and eaten it!

Anyone watching the bat might have thought he was flying aimlessly. He seemed to be darting, swooping, and wheeling in all directions. Actually, he was catching insects as fast as they crossed his path—as many as fifteen or twenty a minute!

The biggest and choicest insects were plump moths. The bat gladly gobbled up those when he found them. But moths weren't always easy to catch. Some moths

could *feel* the sound vibrations the bat sent out. Then they would try to escape.

A moth that felt the bat's vibrations would dodge and veer and zig-zag. It might suddenly fold its wings and let itself drop straight down, almost to the ground. At the last moment, it would swoop into some bushes and hide. Often, the bat couldn't catch moths that did such "tricks."

Other kinds of moths had a different way of escaping. When they felt the bat's sound vibrations come at them, they quickly sent back vibrations of their own. When these reached the bat's ears, he turned aside at once and let the moth go on its way. The bat had learned that moths that made those sounds weren't good to eat. Their vibrations meant, "Don't eat me—I taste bad!"

Although the bat missed some moths, and let others go, he still managed to catch plenty of insects. By the time he started back toward the cave, he was comfortably full. All night long, he had hunted in a world of darkness. But by using sounds, the bat "saw" things as clearly as if they were in bright light!

A bat's way of using echoes to "see" things is known as echolocation. Actually, bats are *not* blind, and can see in daylight. But by being able to hunt in darkness, they have an enormous food supply that they don't have to share with many other creatures.

Putting sound to work

What makes sounds like a violin, a singer, and a big brass band? A phonograph, of course. It makes the sounds you hear from the records you play.

This machine is cutting the sound grooves in a blank record. Thousands of copies will be made from this record.

A phonograph record is made the same way it's played—with a needle. The needle is used to cut the long, winding groove in the surface of the record.

When the record is made, the microphone changes the sound vibrations into patterns of strong and weak electric signals. The signals are sent to an electromagnet next to the record-cutting needle. There they make strong and weak pulls—and the pulls make the needle vibrate. So as the record turns, the needle cuts a groove with a wiggly pattern exactly like the vibrations in the sound.

When you play a record, the phonograph changes the pattern back into sounds. The wiggly groove makes the record needle vibrate. The vibrating needle makes an electromagnet give off patterns of electric signals. The strong and weak electric signals make the phonograph speaker vibrate—and you hear the sounds.

Stereophonic records are made in the same way—but the record-cutting needle copies two kinds of sounds at once. Two electromagnets make the cutting needle vibrate in two different directions and cut different wiggles in each side of the groove.

When you play the stereo record, the needle picks up both sets of wiggles. It sends one set of signals to each speaker—and your ears hear two slightly different sounds that make the music seem "real."

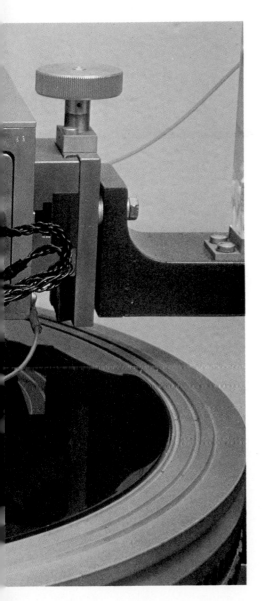

More
Things
That Work

Home computers help people learn—they give directions, ask questions, and check answers. This child has a math program on the computer.

A machine that helps you think

If you're an astronaut in a speeding spaceship, you have a problem. The ship is rocketing through space at tremendous speed—thousands of miles an hour. To change direction, you have to figure out where the ship is and how fast it's traveling—and you have only seconds to do it!

You can't think that fast. But a computer can. A computer is a high-speed thinking machine. It can do the figuring for you and tell you where the ship is—*every* second.

Is the computer smarter than you are? Not really. It doesn't "think" the same way you do. A computer has to be told exactly how to think and what to think about. It can't help you fly a spaceship, run a bank, or find a library book unless someone gives it the right information.

People who work with computers write *programs* for them. They figure out exactly what problems a computer needs to solve. Then they give step-by-step instructions for solving the problems. The computer stores the instructions in its *memory*.

People also figure out exactly what facts the computer needs to know to solve problems. Millions of these facts are also stored in the computer's memory.

When someone gives the computer a problem to solve, it searches its memory for the facts it needs. Then it follows its program and solves the problem step by step. It may go through hundreds of steps to solve a single problem—but it whizzes through those steps in just a few seconds. It saves work—and it saves time, too.

Put-together things

Are your shoes made of leather? Is your sweater made of wool? Are your glasses really glass? Maybe—and maybe not. Any of these things could be plastics.

But what are plastics? They don't grow as plants, like cotton. And they don't grow on animals, like wool. Plastics are made from coal, oil, and other materials. The materials are broken apart in factories, and the molecules of the materials are put back together to make new kinds of materials we call plastics.

These put-together molecules make plastics useful for many things. Plastics can be made into thread for cloth. They can be made into materials that are like leather, or rubber, or unbreakable glass. They can be made nearly as tough and hard as metal, or as soft as silk. And the put-together molecules won't rust, rot, or fall apart as most materials do. Plastics will last for years and years.

But that's the problem with plastics. When most materials are thrown away, they break up and become part of the soil. But things made of plastics last and last. It's hard to get rid of them!

A glass made of glass would break—but this plastic glass bounces.

Machines melt and squeeze tiny beads of plastic into special shapes (left). Workers then put the pieces together to make plastic toys (above).

An airplane pushed by gas

Have you ever wondered why certain kinds of airplanes are called *jet* planes? The word *jet* means a stream of something that's shot out of an opening. And that's how a jet plane flies—by squirting out jets of burning gas.

Instead of propellers, jet planes have engines with spinning parts inside. These fanlike parts scoop in tremendous amounts of air and squeeze the air into a closed space.

Squeezing the air makes it hot. So when the fuel is squirted in, the hot fuel-and-air mixture begins to burn. The hot, burning gases can escape in only one direction—out the back of the engine. As they rush

This jet engine is having a checkup. Airplane mechanics will make repairs and test the engine to be sure it runs smoothly.

backward, they push the plane forward and make it fly.

Many jet planes fly almost as fast as sound travels. And some of the newest jets *are* supersonic (soo puhr SAHN ihk)—they fly faster than sound. They can fly at 1,550 miles (2,494 kilometers) per hour—more than twice as fast as an ordinary jet.

But the bigger and faster the jet planes get, the more room they need to take off and land. So as jet planes get larger, many airports have to be made larger, too.

And, of course, jet planes make noise and fumes. So when new airports are built, they need to be planned carefully. The planners try to make sure that big planes landing and taking off are not a danger or a bother to people who live or work near the airport.

Putting atoms to work

What makes the electricity for your home? It comes from buildings called power plants. In most places, power plants use energy from coal, oil, or gas to make electricity. But some power plants use a different kind of energy— nuclear (NOO klee uhr), or atomic, energy.

Dangerous radiation may leak from a nuclear power plant—so these workers test the area around the plant to make sure it is safe. The suits, gloves, and masks protect them while they work.

Nuclear energy is made by breaking apart the center, or nucleus, of a certain kind of atom—usually uranium (yu RAY nee uhm). When uranium atoms break apart, they give off heat energy. This energy is used to make steam. And the steam runs the generators—the machines that make electricity.

Most power plants burn tremendous amounts of fuel. So power plants that use nuclear energy save a lot of coal, oil, or gas.

But there are problems with nuclear energy, too. Uranium atoms are radioactive (RAY dee oh AK tihv)—they give off rays that are dangerous to living things. Scientists and engineers have to make sure that radioactivity doesn't get out of the power plant and into the air, water, or soil.

The uranium in a nuclear power plant is surrounded by heavy walls of steel and concrete to protect people from the rays. And the atoms are broken apart bit by bit, so that the uranium does not overheat. If it did overheat, it could melt or crack the walls, and the dangerous rays would escape. Even though the uranium is handled very carefully, many people worry about possible accidents.

And when uranium atoms are broken up, radioactive waste is left. This waste stays radioactive for thousands of years! Safe ways have to be found to store the waste from the used-up uranium, so that people won't be hurt by the dangerous rays.

Pictures that fool your eyes

Do you know that a "movie" doesn't really move? Your eyes make it look as if it's moving!

A movie is made with a camera that takes pictures very fast—twenty-four pictures in a second. Each picture is just like a picture taken by an ordinary camera. If a running dog is in the movie, the camera takes a "still" picture of each of the dog's movements.

When the pictures are developed, they are all in a row on a long strip of film. Because the pictures were taken so quickly, each one shows only a few tiny differences from the picture before it.

The film is shown with a projector (pruh JEHK tuhr)—a machine that shines light through the film and onto a screen. Every second, twenty-four pictures flash in front of you. The pictures change so rapidly that you can't possibly see each one by itself or notice the tiny differences. So your eyes blend the pictures into a single picture that "moves."

Cartoons fool your eyes in the same way other movies do. Each picture in the cartoon is drawn and colored by hand. To make the movie, the pictures are photographed in order. In each picture, the characters are standing or moving just a little differently

Each picture, or frame, in this strip of film shows the characters in slightly different positions. When the cartoon is shown on a screen, the pictures flash by very rapidly and the characters seem to move.

than in the one before it. So, when the cartoon is shown, you see the characters "move" as if they were real.

Air traffic controllers use radar to direct planes
near busy airports. The moving spots of light
on the radar screen show where each plane is.

Finding moving things

Airplanes get into traffic jams just as cars do—especially around a busy airport. But people called air traffic controllers can tell where each plane is. They use radar (RAY dahr) to help them direct air traffic.

Radar helps the controllers find planes that are too far away to see. And it does this at night and in rain, fog, or snow.

A radar set sends out radio waves, much like the signals a radio station sends. The radio waves travel in a narrow beam that sweeps around and around in a circle. When the waves hit a flying plane, they bounce back to the radar set. This makes spots of light appear on a special screen.

By following the moving spots of light, a controller can tell how far away a plane is, how high it is, how fast it is flying, and which way it is going. Then the controllers can direct air traffic, much as police officers direct cars. They can make sure that each plane follows a safe path to take off or to land.

Radar is used to watch other moving things, too—even the weather. When a radar beam bounces off the drops of water in storm clouds, it creates a weather picture. Weather forecasters can tell how big a storm is, the direction in which it is moving, and its speed. Then people can get ready for the storm—and airplanes can fly around it safely.

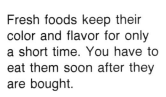
Fresh foods keep their color and flavor for only a short time. You have to eat them soon after they are bought.

Frozen food

Is your piece of apple pie homemade, or did it come frozen? Sometimes it's hard to tell. Frozen foods and fresh foods can look and taste almost the same.

Freezing is a good way to preserve (prih ZUHRV), or save, most foods. It keeps the foods from spoiling, and it keeps their color and flavor from changing. So foods that are frozen don't have to be used right away. They can be kept until you need them.

Foods look and taste better if they are frozen very fast. So frozen foods are prepared in a special way. Usually they are sealed in packages or placed on special trays. Then they are loaded into a huge, extra-cold freezer. Cold air or a cold gas blows over the

Frozen foods will look
and taste much like fresh
foods when they are cooked
—even after weeks or
months in the freezer.

foods and freezes them very quickly, so that
the flavor doesn't change. Or, if the food is in
cans, it is given a bath in a very cold liquid to
make it freeze.

Frozen foods come in handy. Stores can
keep them for a long time—so you can buy
frozen fruits and vegetables all year round.
And frozen foods make cooking easier and
quicker, because some of the work has been
done for you. A can of frozen orange juice is
already squeezed from the oranges, so all you
do is the mixing. And a frozen apple pie is
already put together, so you only bake it.

Many homemade foods can be frozen, too,
if they are tightly sealed or wrapped. This
way, people can cook a number of special
dishes when they have time, and then enjoy
them later.

An elevator car hangs on steel cables inside a shaft. A pulley turns the cables to make the car slide up or down.

An up-down machine

Climbing the stairs in a house is easy. But in a tall building with many floors, it's hard work! People need a better way to get up to the top floors and then down again. This "better way" is an elevator.

An elevator is really a lifting machine. In England and some other countries, that's what it's called—a *lift*. The invention of the elevator has made it possible for people to build and use skyscrapers.

The elevator is like a small room that can be raised and lowered. Strong steel ropes, called cables (KAY buhlz), pull the car up and lower it down. And steel tracks, or guide rails, keep the car from swinging sideways.

The cables are attached to the top and bottom of the elevator car. Then they are wound around large pulleys at the top and bottom of the building to make a strong, tight loop.

The car hangs on one side of the loop. On the other side, the cables are connected to a heavy weight. The hanging weight pulls against the weight of the car. This makes it easier to move the car.

When someone presses the elevator button, an electric signal is sent to a motor at the top of the shaft. The motor turns the top pulley and makes the cables move.

If the pulley is turned one way, the weight is lowered and the car moves up. If it is turned the other way, the weight is raised and the car moves down. The pulley keeps turning and the cables keep moving until the car reaches the right floor. Then the motor stops, and the car doors open so that people can get on or off the elevator.

An oven that stays cool

Could you bake a potato in an oven that doesn't get hot? Yes, you could, if it's a microwave oven. In minutes, the potato gets steaming hot, but the oven stays cool! And the glass or china dishes you cook in stay cool, too.

Micro- means "small." And that's what microwaves are—small radio waves. These waves are so short that they easily penetrate (PEHN uh trayt), or pass into, all kinds of foods.

When the oven is turned on, a special electric tube begins sending out microwaves. On their way into the oven, the microwaves pass through a stirrer, which is like an electric fan. The stirrer scatters the waves, so that they bounce off the metal walls of the oven.

The bouncing microwaves penetrate the food from all directions and make the food molecules move faster and faster. The moving molecules create friction, and the friction produces heat. So the food in the oven warms up immediately, inside and out. In a short time, it's cooked all the way through.

In an ordinary oven, food is heated from the outside. The heat has to move into the food. Because microwaves create heat *inside* the food, a microwave oven cooks food much

Foods cook fast in microwave ovens. In a busy restaurant, a meal is hot and ready to serve in minutes.

faster than a gas or electric oven. So a microwave oven saves time. It bakes a potato in a few minutes instead of an hour—and it heats a hot dog in seconds!

But microwaves can't do some of the things heat can do. They can't make foods crisp or crusty or brown on the outside. So for sizzling meat, crusty bread, and crisp cookies, people use a gas or electric oven that cooks with heat. Or, they use a microwave oven with a special heater. It heats up for a short time and "toasts" the food after the microwaves have cooked it through.

Books to Read

If you like reading about how things work, you'll find lots of good science books to enjoy. A few of them are listed below. Your school or your public library will have many others.

Ages 5 to 8

Adventures with a Cardboard Tube by Harry Milgrom (Dutton, 1972)
Cardboard tubes and a few easy-to-get materials are all you need to do some interesting experiments with light, sound, gravity, and motion.

Energy and Inertia by Hal Hellman (M. Evans, 1970)
Energy can be used and stored, but it can't be made. This book tells why—and it also tells how inertia keeps moving things moving and still things still.

Energy from the Sun by Melvin Berger (Crowell, 1976)
Almost all of the energy we use comes from the sun. The author explains what sunlight does for living things and tells about some new ways people have found to use the sun's energy.

Fire by Gail Kay Haines (Morrow, 1975)
When you breathe and when a fire burns, some of the same things happen. This book tells what fire is and shows how people use fire to do work.

Gravity Is a Mystery by Franklyn M. Branley (T. Y. Crowell, 1970)
We don't know exactly what gravity is, but we know what it does. Here is an explanation of how gravity affects you on earth—and how it would affect you on other planets, too.

Heat and Temperature by Jeanne Bendick (Franklin Watts, 1974)
Heat warms you up—and it makes you cooler, too. Easy experiments will help you find out what heat is, how it moves, and how it makes things change.

High Sounds, Low Sounds by Franklyn M. Branley (T. Y. Crowell, 1967)
You hear sounds when something vibrates. This book shows you where to look for the vibrations and how to make sounds with vibrating things.

The Lever and the Pulley by Hal Hellman (M. Evans, 1971)
Here is an explanation of two simple machines that are used to lift and move things. The pictures help to show how they make a job easier or faster.

Light and Shadow by Carol Schwalberg (Parents, 1972)
Having fun with shadows, mirrors, and water can help you understand what light is and how light waves travel.

Matter All Around You: Solids, Liquids, and Gases by R. J. Lefkowitz (Parents, 1972)
Solids, liquids, and gases are alike in some ways and different in others. The author explains what matter is, what happens when you blow up a balloon or sit in a tub of water, and why you can't walk through a wall.

Science Fun for You in a Minute or Two by Herman and Nina Schneider (McGraw-Hill, 1975)
Here are some quick and easy experiments you can do while you brush your teeth or eat lunch—or sleep!

Science Games and Puzzles by Laurence B. White, Jr. (Addison-Wesley, 1975)
Can you listen with your teeth? This

book will tell you how to do it—and how to do other interesting experiments with things you have at home.

The Shape of Water by Augusta Goldin (Doubleday, 1979)
Playing with water and doing some easy experiments will help you find out how liquids behave and how the molecules of a liquid move.

Streamlined by John Kaufman (Crowell, 1974)
Some shapes move through water and air more easily than others. Activities in this book show you why certain shapes are best for planes, boats, rockets, and race cars.

What Is a Shadow? by Bob Ridiman (Parents, 1973)
Here are some things you can make and do to find out about shadows, electricity, mirrors, and gravity.

Where Does the Garbage Go? by Paul Showers (Crowell, 1974)
People have to get rid of things they can't use. This book tells what happens to garbage—and how some kinds of materials can be used again.

Who Will Drown the Sound? by Carleen May Hutchins (Coward, 1972)
Little sounds and big sounds, added together, can make more noise than your ears can handle. This book tells how sounds are made, how much sound is safe for your ears, and what can be done to protect people from unwanted sounds.

Why Things Work: A Book About Energy by Jeanne Bendick (Parents, 1972)
Nothing starts, stops, or changes without energy. The author tells where we get energy, how we use it, and why we should try to save energy whenever we can.

Ages 9 to 12

Bet You Can't: Science Impossibilities to Fool You by Vicki Cobb (Lothrop, 1980)
Leakproof holes and other impossibilities are tricks you can perform with help from gravity and other forces.

The Bicycle and How It Works by David Inglis Urquhart (Walck, 1972)
The bicycle is a machine that moves something—you. Here is a book that shows how pedals, gears, brakes, and handle bars work and how bicycles have been improved since the first models were built.

Biography of an Atom by J. Bronowski and Millicent E. Selsam (Harper and Row, 1965)
Atoms have a "life history," just as people do. This account traces the history of a single carbon atom through millions of years, from its birth in a star to its place in your body.

Chemistry and Cooking by Philip B. Carona (Prentice-Hall, 1975)
Everything you eat is made of solids, liquids, and gases combined in different ways. These experiments show you what happens when food cooks.

Concoctions by Lowi Price and Marilyn Wronsky (Dutton, 1976)
Other things besides food can come out of your kitchen. Here are recipes for soap, perfume, invisible ink, and other things you can make at home. The directions will tell you exactly how to make and use them safely.

The Dangers of Noise by Lucy Kavaler (Crowell, 1978)
Sound affects your ears every minute of the day—even while you sleep. The author explains how noise can be controlled—and why it should be.

The First Book of Electricity by Sam and Beryl Epstein (Revised Edition, Franklin Watts, 1977)
Clear descriptions of how an electric current is made, transmitted, and put to work in your home are followed by instructions for several safe experiments.

Heat by Vicki Cobb (Franklin Watts, 1973)
People use heat in many ways—yet it took hundreds of years for scientists to discover what heat really is. The author tells how these discoveries were made and shows how heat affects your life.

Hot and Cold by Irving Adler (Revised Edition, John Day, 1975)
How hot and how cold can things get? The author explains what happens to atoms and molecules at very high and very low temperatures, how these temperatures are created, and what instruments are used to measure them.

How Did We Find Out About Electricity? by Isaac Asimov (Walker, 1973)
Careful experiments, clever guesses, and some lucky accidents helped early scientists discover how to make electricity work for people. The author tells how and what these scientists learned about a puzzling form of energy.

How Did We Find Out About Nuclear Power? by Isaac Asimov (Walker, 1976)
The search for nuclear power lasted more than a hundred years. This is the story of the many people whose careful work released the energy in the atom.

Inventions That Made History by David C. Cooke (Putnam, 1968)
Sewing machines and X rays, typewriters and television all came about when people needed better ways to do things. Here are brief stories of some important inventions and the people who made them.

Light: Color and Life for the World by Frederick C. Huber (McKay, 1978)
Why do we need light? This book answers the question and provides some fascinating information about light and how light affects living things.

Look in the Mirror by Sam and Beryl Epstein (Holiday, 1973)
Mirrors can reflect things in very interesting ways. You can use straight and curved mirrors to see the back of your head, look around corners, or give your reflection a funny shape.

The Paper Airplane Book by Seymour Simon (Viking, 1971)
Making your own paper planes can help you find out how real planes lift, turn, and hold a steady course. The book includes patterns for straight gliders, acrobatic planes, and a "flying wing."

Scientists and Their Discoveries by Tillie S. Pine and Joseph Levine (McGraw-Hill, 1978)
These stories of famous scientists and some of their discoveries are followed by easy activities that show you how their ideas worked.

The Simple Facts of Simple Machines by Elizabeth James and Carol Barkin (Lothrop, 1975)
Hammers and doorknobs and stadium ramps all are simple machines. The photographs and diagrams in this book show how machines make work easier.

They Said It Couldn't Be Done by Ross Olney (Dutton, 1979)
Bridges and subways, dams and trips to the moon—here are stories of ten "impossible" accomplishments and the people who made them possible.

New Words

Here are some of the words you have met in this book. Many of them may be new to you, but all of them are used in science. Next to each word you'll see how to say the word: absorb (ab SAWRB). The part shown in capital letters is said a little more loudly than the rest of the word. One or two sentences under each word tell what the word means.

absorb (ab SAWRB)
Absorb means "take in" or "soak up." Things get warm when they absorb heat.

atom (AT uhm)
An atom is the smallest possible bit of an element. All things are made from atoms. *See also* **element.**

axle (AK suhl)
An axle is a rod on which a wheel turns.

carbon (KAHR buhn)
Carbon is an element. Usually it is a crumbly or powdery black material. Coal is mostly carbon. *See also* **element.**

chemical (KEHM uh kuhl) **energy**
Chemical energy is energy given off when different kinds of matter change or combine. The chemical energy stored in wood is changed to heat when the wood burns.

compound (KAHM pownd)
A compound is matter made when atoms of two or more different elements join together. Water is a compound of hydrogen and oxygen. *See also* **element.**

computer (kuhm PYOO tuhr)
A computer is a machine that stores information and uses it to solve problems and do other jobs.

condense (kuhn DEHNS)
Condense means "change from a gas to a liquid." Steam condenses to water when it cools.

conduct (kuhn DUHKT)
Conduct means "carry." Some kinds of matter conduct heat, sound, or electricity very well.

contract (kuhn TRAKT)
Contract means "shrink." When things contract, they take up less space.

current (KUR uhnt) **electricity**
Current electricity is a steady flow of electricity through a wire. *See also* **static electricity.**

cylinder (SIHL uhn duhr)
In an engine, a cylinder is a hollow tube in which the fuel burns. *See also* **piston.**

diaphragm (DY uh fram)
In a camera, the diaphragm is the part that controls the amount of light that gets to the film. A diaphragm is also a thin sheet of material that conducts sound.

electromagnet (ih LEHK troh MAG niht)
An electromagnet is a magnet made by sending electricity through a wire wound around a piece of iron.

electron (ih LEHK trahn)
An electron is a tiny part of an atom. Electrons carry a small amount of electricity.

element (EHL uh muhnt)
An element is matter that contains only one kind of atom. Gold and iron are elements.

energy (EHN uhr jee)
Energy is anything that can make things work. Heat, light, and electricity are kinds of energy.

engine (EHN juhn)
An engine is a machine that uses energy to make other machines, or parts of machines, move or do work.

evaporate (ih VAP uh rayt)
Evaporate means "change from a liquid to a gas." Water evaporates when it boils away.

expand (ehk SPAND)
Expand means "get larger." When things expand, they take up more space.

filament (FIHL uh muhnt)
A filament is the thin, threadlike wire that gives off light in a burning light bulb.

focus (FOH kuhs)
Focus means "meet in a point." Some lenses make light rays focus.

force (fawrs)
A force is anything that makes objects move or stop moving.

frequency (FREE kwuhn see)
Frequency is how often something happens in a certain amount of time, such as an hour or a second.

friction (FRIHK shuhn)
Friction is the rubbing created when something moves across or through a solid, liquid, or gas.

fuel (FYOO uhl)
Fuel is matter that is burned to produce heat or to make machines run. Coal, oil, and gasoline are fuels.

gas (gas)
Gas is one of the three forms of matter. In a gas, the molecules spread apart in all directions to fill up space. Air is a gas. *See also* **liquid; solid.**

gear (gihr)
A gear is a wheel with teeth on the edge. The teeth can push on the teeth of another gear to make it move.

generator (JEHN uh ray tuhr)
A generator is a machine that makes electricity.

gravity (GRAV uh tee)
Gravity is the force that pulls things toward the earth.

hologram (HAHL uh gram)
A hologram is a photograph taken with laser light.

hydrogen (HY druh juhn)
Hydrogen is an element. It is a gas with no color or smell. *See also* **element.**

inclined plane (ihn KLYND PLAYN)
An inclined plane is a slanted, flat surface.

inertia (ihn UR shuh)
Inertia is the name given to the way still objects stay still unless an outside force makes them move, and moving objects keep moving unless an outside force makes them stop.

infrared (IHN fruh REHD) **ray**
An infrared ray is like a light ray, but it is invisible and it produces heat.

insulate (IHN suh layt)
Insulate means "surround." Insulated things are surrounded with a material that keeps energy from moving in or out.

inventor (ihn VEHN tuhr)
An inventor is a person who thinks out and makes new things.

kinetic (kih NEHT ihk) **energy**
Kinetic energy is the energy things have when they are moving. When a ball is thrown, it has kinetic energy.

laser (LAY zuhr) **beam**
A laser beam is a special kind of light. The laser beam is very narrow and can be very powerful.

lens (lehnz)
A lens is a curved, clear piece of glass or other material like that in a pair of glasses. A lens bends any light that passes through it.

lever (LEHV uhr)
A lever is a bar used to move a load. Pushing or pulling one end of the lever makes the load move.

liquid (LIHK wihd)
Liquid is one of the three forms of matter. In a liquid, the molecules move around each other but do not spread apart in all directions. Water is a liquid. *See also* **solid; gas.**

magnet (MAG niht)
A magnet is a piece of iron, steel, or stone having a force that pulls on iron or steel.

magnetism (MAG nuh tihz uhm)
Magnetism is the force that is in a magnet.

magnifying (MAG nuh fy ihng) **glass**
A magnifying glass is a lens that makes things look larger.

matter (MAT uhr)
Matter is what all things are made of. Matter has weight and takes up space. *See also* **gas; liquid; solid.**

memory (MEHM uhr ee)
The memory is the part of a computer in which information is stored.

microphone (MY kruh fohn)
A microphone is an instrument that changes sounds into electric signals.

microscope (MY kruh skohp)
A microscope is an instrument with lenses that make very small things look larger.

microwave (MY kroh WAYV)
A microwave is a very short radio wave that produces heat.

mirage (muh RAHZH)
A mirage is a view of an object or scene that is not where it appears to be.

molecule (MAHL uh kyool)
A molecule is a particle of matter formed when two or more atoms are joined together. *See also* **atom.**

nuclear (NOO klee uhr) **energy**
Nuclear energy is energy produced by splitting the nucleus of certain kinds of atoms. *See also* **nucleus.**

nucleus (NOO klee uhs)
The nucleus is the heavy center part of an atom.

oxygen (AHK suh juhn)
Oxygen is an element. It is a colorless, odorless gas that is part of the air. *See also* **element.**

penetrate (PEHN uh trayt)
Penetrate means "get into or through." Food cooks when heat penetrates it.

percussion (puhr KUHSH uhn) **instrument**
A percussion instrument is a musical instrument that is played by striking or hitting it. A drum is a percussion instrument.

perpetual (puhr PEHCH u uhl) **motion**
Perpetual motion is motion that keeps going forever once it is started. Perpetual motion cannot actually be created.

photon (FOH tahn)
A photon is a bit of light energy.

piston (PIHS tuhn)
A piston is a metal piece that moves back and forth inside the cylinder of an engine. *See also* **cylinder.**

plastics (PLAS tihks)
Plastics are man-made materials that are easily shaped. They are made from coal, oil, or other substances.

pole (POHL)
A pole is a part of a magnet where the force is strongest.

potential (puh TEHN shuhl) **energy**
Potential energy is the energy stored in something that is not yet moving, but that can move.

prism (PRIHZ uhm)
A prism is a clear piece of glass with slanted, flat sides. Light shining through a prism separates into different colors.

program (PROH gram)
A program is a set of instructions a computer uses to solve problems.

pulley (PUL ee)
A pulley is a wheel with a grooved rim through which a rope or cable runs. Pulleys are used to lift loads.

radar (RAY dahr)
A radar is an instrument that uses reflected radio waves to locate unseen planes and other objects.

radioactive (RAY dee oh AK tihv)
Radioactive means "giving off rays." Radioactive atoms give off energy as they break apart.

ray (ray)
A ray is a line or beam of energy, such as light or heat.

reflect (rih FLEHKT)
Reflect means "give back." A mirror reflects light.

resist (rih ZIHST)
Resist means "act against." Some kinds of wire resist the flow of electricity more than others.

retina (REHT uh nuh)
The retina is the spot at the back of the eye that is sensitive to light.

satellite (SAT uh lyt)
A satellite is an object that revolves in space around the earth or another planet.

shutter (SHUHT uhr)
In a camera, the shutter is the part that opens and closes to expose the film to light.

solar (SOH luhr)
Solar means "of the sun." Solar energy is energy from the sun.

solid (SAHL ihd)
Solid is one of the three forms of matter. In a solid, the molecules hold together and do not move freely. Glass is a solid. *See also* **gas; liquid.**

sonar (SOH nahr)
Sonar is an instrument that uses sound to locate underwater objects.

source (sawrs)
A source is a place from which something comes.

static (STAT ihk) **electricity**
Static electricity is electricity that builds up on a person or object. Static electricity on a person's body can cause a shock when metal is touched. *See also* **current electricity.**

stereophonic (STEHR ee uh FAHN ihk)
Stereophonic means "giving lifelike sound." Stereophonic sound comes from two or more speakers placed apart from each other.

supersonic (SOO puhr SAHN ihk)
Supersonic means "faster than sound travels." Supersonic planes fly faster than the speed of sound.

telescope (TEHL uh skohp)
A telescope is an instrument that makes faraway things appear closer.

transparent (trans PAIR uhnt)
Transparent means "easily seen through." The air and most window glass are transparent.

tungsten (TUHNG stuhn)
Tungsten is an element. It is a grayish metal that does not melt easily. *See also* **element.**

ultrasound (UHL truh sownd)
Ultrasound is sound higher than human ears can hear.

ultraviolet (UHL truh VY uh liht) **ray**
An ultraviolet ray is an invisible light wave that causes sunburn.

uranium (yu RAY nee uhm)
Uranium is an element. It is a heavy, radioactive metal. *See also* **element, radioactive.**

valve (valv)
A valve is a moving part that opens and closes a pipe or tube.

vapor (VAY puhr)
A vapor is a gas formed when something is heated. Steam is water vapor.

vibrate (VY brayt)
Vibrate means "move back and forth rapidly." Sounds are made by things that vibrate.

vocal cords (VOH kuhl KAWRDZ)
Vocal cords are thin pieces of body tissue inside the throat that vibrate to make voice sounds.

wave (wayv)
A wave is a regular movement of something. Energy travels in waves.

wedge (wehj)
A wedge is a shape with one narrow edge used to cut, split, or push through something.

X ray (EHKS ray)
An X ray is a very short, invisible wave of energy that can pass through soft parts of the body.

Illustration acknowledgments

The publishers of *Childcraft* gratefully acknowledge the courtesy of the following photographers, agencies, and organizations for illustrations in this volume. When all the illustrations for a sequence of pages are from a single source, the inclusive page numbers are given. In all other instances, the page numbers refer to facing pages, which are considered as a single unit or spread. All illustrations are the exclusive property of the publishers of *Childcraft* unless names are marked with an asterisk (*).

4–5:	Stan Smetkowski, *Childcraft* photo
6–9:	Robert Byrd
10–11:	*Childcraft* photo; Jack Wallen
12–13:	Robert Byrd
14–15:	*Childcraft* photo
16–17:	NASA
18–19:	*Childcraft* photo by Daniel D. Miller
20–21:	Robert Byrd
22–23:	Stan Smetkowski, *Childcraft* photo
24–25:	Eulala Conner
26–27:	David Wiesner
28–29:	Bernard Arendt*; *Childcraft* photo by Gilbert Meyers; *Childcraft* photo; *Childcraft* photo by Daniel D. Miller
30–31:	David Wiesner
32–33:	Eulala Conner
34–35:	Sven Samelius*; Energy Research and Development Administration*; Duane Bradford, Black Star*; Edward Pieratt, Black Star*
36–37:	Eulala Conner
38–39:	David Wiesner
40–41:	*Childcraft* photo
42–43:	Kathy Clo
44–45:	David Wiesner
46–51:	Christine di Monda
52–53:	Christine di Monda; *Childcraft* photo
54–55:	The Kirby Company*; Kathy Clo
56–57:	Stan Smetkowski, *Childcraft* photo
58–59:	Robert Byrd
60–61:	*Childcraft* photo; Jack Wallen
62–63:	*Childcraft* photo
64–65:	Stella Ormai
66–67:	*Childcraft* photo
68–69:	Stella Ormai; *Childcraft* photo
70–71:	*Childcraft* photo
72–75:	Robert Byrd
76–77:	Stella Ormai
78–87:	Michael Hague
88–89:	Michael Hague; Robert Byrd
90–91:	*Childcraft* photo
92–93:	Stella Ormai
94–95:	Robert Byrd
96–97:	*Childcraft* photo
98–99:	Stan Smetkowski, *Childcraft* photo
100–101:	Kathy Clo
102–103:	Stella Ormai; Jack Wallen
104–105:	*Childcraft* photo
106–109:	Stella Ormai
110–111:	Kathy Clo
112–113:	*Childcraft* photo by Daniel D. Miller
114–117:	*Childcraft* photo
118–125:	Friso Henstra
126–127:	*Childcraft* photo by Daniel D. Miller
128–129:	Kathy Clo
130–131:	Stan Smetkowski, *Childcraft* photo
132–133:	Robert Byrd
134–135:	Brian Cody
136–137:	*Childcraft* photo
138–139:	Robert Byrd; Kathy Clo
140–143:	Brian Cody
144–145:	*Childcraft* photo
146–147:	Robert Byrd
148–149:	Kathy Clo; *Childcraft* photo

150–151: Brian Cody; *Childcraft* photo
152–153: Brian Cody
154–155: *Childcraft* photo
156–157: Kathy Clo
158–165: Kinuko Craft
166–167: *Childcraft* photo; Robert Byrd
168–169: *Childcraft* photo
170–171: Stan Smetkowski, *Childcraft* photo
172–173: Kathy Clo
174–175: Artstreet*
176–179: *Childcraft* photo
180–181: David Wiesner
182–183: *Childcraft* photo; Jack Wallen
184–185: *Childcraft* photo by Daniel D. Miller
186–187: Kathy Clo; Jack Wallen
188–189: Dennis di Cicco*; Stella Ormai
190–191: *Childcraft* photo; Mark Rosenthal, Van Cleve Photography*; Jack Wallen
192–193: David Wiesner; Jack Wallen
194–195: *Childcraft* photo
196–197: Herbert Matter, BASF Wyandotte Corporation*
198–199: Jack Wallen
200–201: David Wiesner
202–203: © Alistair B. Fraser*
204–205: Eulala Conner
206–211: Friso Henstra
212–213: David Wiesner
214–215: Museum of the Fine Arts Research and Holographic Center (*Childcraft* photo)
216–217: Jack Wallen; Gregory Houghton*
218–219: Kathy Clo
220–221: Stan Smetkowski, *Childcraft* photo
222–223: Eulala Conner
224–225: Stella Ormai
226–227: Eulala Conner; *Childcraft* photo
228–229: *Childcraft* photo
230–231: Stella Ormai
232–223: Eulala Conner
234–237: *Childcraft* photo
238–243: Christine di Monda
244–245: Brent Jones*
246–247: *Childcraft* photo
248–249: Stella Ormai; Kathy Clo
250–251: Eulala Conner; *Childcraft* photo
252–253: Kathy Clo
254–255: Stan Smetkowski, *Childcraft* photo
256–257: Robert Byrd
258–261: Stella Ormai
262–263: *Childcraft* photo; Kathy Clo
264–267: Robert Byrd
268–269: Stella Ormai
270–271: *Childcraft* photo
272–273: Robert Byrd
274–281: *Childcraft* photo
282–283: *Childcraft* photo; Robert Byrd
284–285: *Childcraft* photo
286–287: Kathy Clo; *Childcraft* photo
288–289: Robert Byrd
290–291: *Childcraft* photo by Marshall Berman
292–293: Robert Byrd
294–299: Michael Hague
300–301: Shure Brothers, Inc. (*Childcraft* photo)
302–303: Stan Smetkowski, *Childcraft* photo
304–305: *Childcraft* photo
306–307: Playskool Inc. (*Childcraft* photo)
308–309: *Childcraft* photo by Marshall Berman
310–311: Levesque, Gamma/Liaison*
312–313: © 1981 United Feature Syndicate*
314–315: Milt and Joan Mann*
316–319: *Childcraft* photo
320–321: L'Escargot (*Childcraft* photo)

Cover: Pamela Ford Johnson

Index

This index is an alphabetical list of the important topics covered in this book. It will help you find information given in both words *and* pictures. To help you understand what an entry means, there is often a helping word in parentheses. For example, **cylinder** (part of engine). If there is information in both words *and* pictures, you will see the words *with pictures* after the page number. If there is *only* a picture, you will see the word *picture* before the page number. If you do not find what you want in this index, please go to the General Index in Volume 15, which is a key to all of the books.